Moral Reflections on
Foreign Policy in a Religious War

Moral Reflections on Foreign Policy in a Religious War

Ronald H. Stone

LEXINGTON BOOKS
A division of
ROWMAN & LITTLEFIELD PUBLISHERS, INC.
Lanham • Boulder • New York • Toronto • Plymouth, UK

LEXINGTON BOOKS

A division of Rowman & Littlefield Publishers, Inc.
A wholly owned subsidary of The Rowman & Littlefield Publishing Group, Inc.
4501 Forbes Boulevard, Suite 200
Lanham, MD 20706

Estover Road
Plymouth PL6 7PY
United Kingdom

British Library Cataloguing in Publication Information Available

Library of Congress Cataloging-in-Publication Data

Stone, Ronald H.
   Moral reflections on foreign policy in a religious war / Ronald H. Stone.
      p. cm.
   Includes bibliographical references (p.   ) and index.
   ISBN-13: 978-0-7391-2737-7 (cloth : alk. paper)
   ISBN-10: 0-7391-2737-3 (cloth : alk. paper)
   ISBN-13: 978-0-7391-2738-4 (pbk. : alk. paper)
   ISBN-10: 0-7391-2738-1 (pbk. : alk. paper)
   1. War—Religious aspects. 2. War—Moral and ethical aspects. 3. Religion and politics.
   4. International relations. 5. Religions—Relations. I. Title. BL65.W2S76 2008
   201'.7273—dc22

                                                                        2008003796

Printed in the United States of America

∞™ The paper used in this publication meets the minimum requirements of
American National Standard for Information Sciences—Permanence of Paper
for Printed Library Materials, ANSI/NISO Z39.48-1992.

To Linda Haddad,

Counselor and Companion

With Love

Related Books by Ronald H. Stone

Edited with Matthew Lon Weaver, *Against the Third Reich* by Paul Tillich
Christian Realism and Peacemaking
Edited, *Faith and Politics* by Reinhold Niebuhr
Paul Tillich's Radical Social Thought
Edited with Dana Wilbanks, *The Peacemaking Struggle: Militarism and Resistance*
Prophetic Realism: Beyond Militarism and Pacifism in an Age of Terror
Realism and Hope
Edited, *Reformed Faith and Politics*
Reinhold Niebuhr: Prophet to Politicians
Edited with Robert L. Stivers, *Resistance and Theological Ethics*
Edited, *Theology of Peace* by Paul Tillich

~

Table of Contents

~

Preface

The thesis of this book is that foreign policy thinkers in the United States must take religion seriously in their analysis of policy conflicts in the Middle East. Secular analysis focusing on only national interest and power politics cannot comprehend the tragedy into which the United States has fallen. Western analyses focusing on democracy miss the point. Suicide bombers and sectarian conflicts between Shia and Sunni forces in Iraq are all rooted in religious conviction. Contemporary Middle Easterners in many cases regard wars to be of religious moment in a way similar to the wars recorded in the same region in the scriptures of Judaism, Islam, and Christianity. Western participants are radically more secular than Middle Eastern Moslems. Ignorance of how religion functions personally or socially is ignorance of a major factor in any Middle East conflict. In 2007 after five years of war the U.S. government admitted it was confronting a civil war in Iraq. It recognized that it had insufficient forces to quell the struggle and that the Iraqis themselves must resolve their war. This shift in American foreign policy thinking was an advance on previous stubborn disregard of issues internal to Iraq. But the U.S. administration as late as the winter of 2007–2008 did not recognize the religious nature of the conflict. The United States was so concerned to deny deep Islamic tendencies toward jihad that it could not articulate the obvious religious aspects of the war.

Most wars have religious dimensions in that religious claims are made by participants in the war. Most people including warriors pray about their deepest concerns regarding life and death. But to say a war is religious is to recognize that the high religious authorities sanction it, and that people include their enemies' religion in their description of their enemy. It is not necessary that all religious authorities sanction it nor is it necessary that all combatants or policy makers recognize its religious nature. Other factors than religion may be involved like gold, oil, national defense, other economic interests, national pride, and so on.

Of course, Shia and Sunni are competing over issues of sovereignty and over oil, but their religious convictions are more fundamental. Their religious convictions related to their history of war divide them and cause neighbor to war on neighbor. The United States is particularly concerned about the oil resources and the nature of the sovereignty of the country and less about ancient religious divisions that predate the United States. Mosques are prime targets in Iraq, and people are executed simply for their religious identification within Islam. Al Qaeda, basically militant Sunni, exploits the religious differences to keep its war against U.S. globalization and presence in the Middle East progressing. While significant Sunni and Shia forces would seek peace, and many would settle for compromise solutions, al Qaeda's interests do not incline it toward peace. Its fight is primarily against U.S. and renewed British presence in the area. Therefore the mistaken appointment of Tony Blair, a British invader and occupier, is doomed to disappointment even before he begins to work toward a resolution of the Israel-Palestine impasse and other issues in the region because jihad is directed against invaders in defense of Islam.

Religious quarrels separate Hamas and Fatah as they suffer under Jewish occupation. Israel's claims for formerly Palestinian land are grounded in perceptions of scriptures and divine will. Hezbollah is in part a religious movement as is Hamas. The religious conflicts and problems divide Americans as well as Arabs. Christian fundamentalists support Israel's occupation and a U.S. policy advancing Israel's occupation for religiously based interpretations of reality. Fundamentalists and evangelical-oriented political campaigns are a necessary part of the Republican Party's strategy, and so even U.S. Presidential elections which lead to choices of foreign policy elites have religious dimensions. Similarly mainline Protestant organizing had an effect in the Ohio elections of 2006. Mainline Protestant church policy statements are often critical of Israel's occupation, and Jewish leaders lobby both Protestant Churches and the government to support Israel's expansion.

The book's argument is that the religious dimensions of the two wars: the first, against terrorists who attack the United States, and the second, within Iraq, have not only general religious dimensions but direct religious origins. Most suicidal terrorists are following religious leadership, and the failure of the U.S. coalition occupation of Iraq is due to the Shia-Sunni religious conflict in the situation.

Ancient authorities often regarded war to be a religious issue whether they reflected Greek, Roman, or Hebrew traditions. The Biblical prophets—Amos, Isaiah, Jeremiah, Micah, Elijah, and Elisha—were experts in both international relations and in religion. Our leadership in both international relations and religion must have wisdom in the other field or fail in leadership. While this book integrates study in international relations and religion it also integrates moral reflection on both. Moral reflection can help purify religion. Moral religion can assist to limit nations from policies driven by fear, pride, and nationalism.

This study includes three chapters on moral thinking about international relations: one on responsive moral reflection, one on just peacemaking theory, and one on just war theory. This moral theory then is applied to the Middle East conflicts with the United States in an argument to reduce the U.S. militarization of its polices for the sake of greater security. Jihad, a fundamental Islamic theory that requires resistance to foreign occupation and the mixture of religious revivalism and occupation, will produce terrorist acts against the United States. Throughout the book interreligious dialogue is seen as a hopeful venture and an aid in reducing the religious contribution to modern warfare.

The study of international relations, in my case, goes back to a course by Professor Albert Sellen at Morningside College in Iowa. This continued with Professors Reinhold Niebuhr and William Fox at Union Theological Seminary and Columbia University including the International Fellows Program, which introduced me to Hans J. Morgenthau in the context of the early days of the Vietnam War. At the time I was assisting Dr. Herman Reissig in his role as Secretary for International Relations in the United Church of Christ. My debt to Professor Roger L. Shinn is enormous as he recommended me for that program and asked me to assist Reinhold Niebuhr in his seminar in retirement. Roger L. Shinn and John C. Bennett, my doctor father, both combined realism and moral sensitivity in a manner I would like to emulate.

Because of my writing on Reinhold Niebuhr's international relations perspective, I was asked to join a task force of the Presbyterian Church on international relations and peacemaking before I became a Presbyterian. This remarkable working group produced a foundation paper *Peacemaking: the Believer's Calling* of which I believe Edward Leroy Long, Jr., then of Oberlin College, and I wrote most of the text. I first proposed we create a program to back up our bold statements. Dean Lewis, the Coordinator of the Advisory Council on Social Policy of the church, requested I prepare a paper on the subject.

When it was proposed we could finance it by a special church offering, the idea of a program took wings and eventually became both policy and program in 1980. Disputes in the Committee over our work had led to reconstituting the Committee and in its second form a remarkable lay woman who had served as President of Presbyterian Women joined the Committee. Mary Pardee's work with the committee was peacemaking and healing. She wrote a poem to preface the paper which utilized the concept of "Kairos" or decisive time which I had introduced to the committee as I was working on writing a book on Paul Tillich's social thought. Twenty-five years later Mary asked me to lecture on ethics and international relations at the Longwood Retirement Community of which she was the continuing education chair. This book grew out of those four lectures and Mary died during the term of those lectures.

In between the time of that task force on international relations and peacemaking and the present crisis in the Middle East, Edward Long, Jr., and I have partnered on other papers and policies for the church on peacemaking, humanitarian intervention to stop genocide, and religion, violence, and terrorism. Partnerships with Dana Wilbanks and Bob Stivers have also produced policy documents for the church to debate and amend on resistance to militarism, theological ethics and resistance, and other subjects. This church participation has led me to revise my theoretical orientation of thinking of international relations as only power politics. Now I try to keep before my mind the imperatives of peacemaking as well.

The church also asked me to participate in a study of peacemaking in the Middle East in 2004 and this led to remarkable dialogues with sheiks, imams, rabbis, prime ministers, foreign ministers, and religious leaders from Baghdad, Amman, Jerusalem, Beirut, Cairo, and Damascus. This complimented the three months I had spent living between Jerusalem and Bethlehem in 1980 and other shorter visits and led through controversy in 2004–2006 to this book. Experiences in Palestine in 2007 with Israelis led to further dialogue and reflection on Biblical theology regarding the land also included in chapter 5. I, of course, do not believe any land is holy, but I know many adherents of three great religions take Palestine as a holy land. I offer up in this study based on realist suppositions recognizing that many aspects of the wars today in the Middle East are religious, and that the United States errs in its policies, in part, because it has not understood that phenomena well. I hope these words can add to the peacemaking processes already at work in the midst of conflicts in that special place.

~

Introduction

On September 11, 2001, I finished a lecture on the relationship of Christianity to politics at Pittsburgh Theological Seminary and, leaving the classroom, entered a noisy hallway. A student there who was called to duty as a National Guard soldier told me: "Professor Stone we are at war." An hour and a half later, after watching TV and revising my chapel service, I led worship in the Seminary chapel. Out of approximately 150 staff, faculty, and students present, forty of these had relatives or close friends who worked either on Wall Street or in the Pentagon. Other seminary students trained as grief counselors were on their way to Shanksville, Pennsylvania, where Flight 93 had crashed. Highrises in downtown Pittsburgh were evacuated, and confusion reigned as the new millennium opened with a religious war. Only months earlier we had hoped for peace dividends in our national budget, for more international order and law, and for disciplined, international, humanitarian intervention to rescue beleaguered civilian populations. Now traumatic struggles which originated in the Middle East came home. There may be no centers in the United States that are more religious than theological seminaries which concentrate full-time on advanced religious learning. In that place the connections to American financial might and military power were very clear as members of a theological community shared stories of relatives and friends at work in the centers of financial and military might whose fates at the time were unknown. In a classroom across the hall a professor had held forth on the religious wars of conquest in the Biblical book of Joshua. Other classes down the hall had focused on the connections between mission work and imperialism and the worldwide ministry and influence of the church. Those witnesses to acquaintances working in the World Trade Center and the Pentagon indicated the close relationship of American religious leadership to war and international financial power.

Kenneth Vaux in his book on the war[1] treats religion as the center of the culture and sees theology providing the basic pictures or paradigms which drive a culture in a certain direction. Certainly American economy reflects the Protestant work ethic while its largest church reflects its origins in the religious world of the Roman Empire. Democracy, human rights, capitalism, and aggressiveness all have their origins in certain views of the meaning of life, grounded in assumptions about the nature of humanity which finally rests in the dimly understood theological presuppositions of a culture. Study after study have shown that the votes of the religious right were necessary to elect the administration that responded to the leadership of a born again president who claimed Jesus as his major guide in political philosophy. Osama bin Laden would in an interview captured on tape interpreted the attack as revenge for martyred Arab children who had thrown rocks at Jews at the site of the Temple. More often he referred to it as one more step in his long campaign against the United States which had neglected the Arab brigade in Afghanistan after using them to drive the Russians out of Afghanistan. He would go on raising his objection against the American armed forces present in Saudi Arabia, the home of the cities he regarded as holy, Medina and Mecca. At a deeper level Osama bin Laden was an opponent of the guardians of those cities, the Saudi clan which America supported and backed. Failing in campaigns to Islamize Arab states, he and allies would hit beyond Arab states at the farther enemy, the United States.

Most wars have a mixture of motivations for the engagements; often religion is one of the ingredients. There are adequate reasons to believe that the struggle in which the United States is engaged in with militant Moslems has deep religious roots. Other factors include bad intelligence about weapons of mass destruction, failures in diplomacy, the psychologies of leading actors, factors of pride, neoconservative ideology, control of oil supplies, revenge, defense of borders, support for particular rulers, and so on. But when U.S. military decisions interact with the religious-civil war in Iraq between Sunni and Shia sects of Islam the religious issues are obviously very important. Any in-depth analysis of the cultures fighting uncovers religious issues at deeper levels. But as the tape on which Osama bin Laden admitted taking credit for and planning the attack on the World Trade Center indicated, the fight over Jerusalem is close to the center of the issue. Saddam Hussein's last broadcast before his arrest blamed the American success in overrunning his armies on

Shia perfidy—echoing a supposed Shia betrayal of Baghdad to the Mongols eight hundred years earlier.

The spirit that moves through the Palestinian people will not accept total Israeli dominance of their lives. The spirit of the Israeli people caught up in defense and insecurity oppresses the Arab peoples they control. Again and again any visitor to the Middle East encounters the overlap of the trifurcated faiths of the region. Egyptians permit Christian pilgrims, and Jews to visit the monastery Emperor Justinian founded, St. Catherine, at the foot of Mount Horeb, possible site both of Mohammed's visit and Moses' reception of the Ten Commandments which guide all three faiths. Or at the Church of the Holy Sepulcher, a Moslem family guards the keys while Israel controls the city. Almost all of the most holy sites of Christendom are under Jewish authority while Israel controls access to Islam's Jerusalem mosques. The United States, home to both Jews and Moslems but dominated by Christians, tilts decisively in favor of Israel against Moslems in those struggles and supplies Israel with modern weaponry and the highest amount of international aid extended to any country. Underlying the whole conflict, of course, are the actions of the United States, with European collaboration, in establishing Israel as a state after the European Holocaust. The Holocaust, itself a bitterly delayed fruit of Christian anti-Judaism, was turned into anti-Semitism within Christendom by modern pagans extolling racist pseudo-science. Fundamental to the conflicts and even bigger in the causative factors of terrorism and war than oil is the reality of the Jewish attempt, financed by America, to secure itself a homeland after the Holocaust. This is all as religious as the Old Testament which is mostly about the Hebrews struggle with a perceived divine blessing to win and control the land of Palestine. This is still the issue: how is control of the land of Palestine to be decided? Especially prominent in the scripture are the Egyptians, the Assyrians, the Babylonians, the Persians, the Greeks, the Syrians, the Lebanese, the Philistines, and all of the little states listed in Amos: Damascus, Gaza, Ashdod, Tyre, Ammon, Gilead, Edom, Moab, Judah, and Israel. In the New Testament, Rome enters the fray. Isaiah expects peace when people honor their God, the nations pursue justice, and there is an agreed upon international code which he expects to come form Zion. The Middle East is as far from this peace as it was in the liberation of the Hebrew slaves from Egypt and their destruction of the inhabitants, cities, and gods in the Holy Land. All three of our holy books—the Koran, the Torah, and the New Testament—support or expect wars.

There is another tradition, too, of seeking peace and justice in all three traditions. Sometimes the wars themselves seek peace and justice. War is not all bad as it can liberate slaves, correct injustices, pull down evil rulers, and so forth, but still it is mostly evil as it destroys the works of humanity, nature, and the people themselves. It also prepares the origins of the next wars in the human traumas inflicted and in the injustices left unresolved by war. The United States did not seek a religious war, but it has found itself in one. Roots of terrorism too are found in religion. Some resources for peace are also found in religion, but just as the causes of even religious wars are not totally about religion so the resolution of those wars we can resolve will not be found only in religion.

The conclusions of the book in chapter 8 will then be a mixture of policy recommendations about religion, morality, and international politics, or in particular, U.S. foreign policy as it participates in international politics. The recommendations will grow out of a particular philosophy which is recognizably American and religious. But the argument of the book will flow through philosophical argument in the three fields of morals, politics, and religion. Though I actively participate in both religion and politics, I was trained as a philosopher of morals, religion, and politics, and that is the perspective the book presents. The book is written for religious people who are willing to learn about the role of international politics in the formation and expression of their religious traditions and also for political people who are willing to learn about the deep effects religious life has upon international politics. I hope both professional leaders of religious communities and professionals in the foreign affairs vocations will learn from the book and that the American public can begin to learn about the dangerous, inevitable intersections between religion and international politics. In a season of religious wars, it makes no sense to act as if religion and international politics are not integrally related.

Outline

The first chapter, "The Relationship of Ethics to International Politics," emphasizes the complexity of the relationship of ethics to international politics and surveys several historical options for relating the two from Thucydides to the moral reasoning about the case of the Iraq war. Then the reflections of three philosophers of international politics on recent U.S. policy are presented. An examination of a typology of theories of international politics leads to a conclusion in the section, "What is going on?," that the primary debate in political theory about the Iraq war can be summarized as a debate between liberationist thinkers among the neoconservatives and realist thinkers among the critics. In moral theory the issue is between optimistic teleologists and more pessimistic responders. The second chapter moves into considering the rules of war in "Just War and Jihad." Fuller consideration of both the Moslem and Christian rules would have inclined a wise American administration to stay out of the responsibilities of waging war to occupy Afghanistan and Iraq. Chapter 3 moves on to consider an important modern theory of morality and foreign policy developed under the title of "Just Peacemaking Theory."[2] I have been deeply associated with the development of this theory, but my critique in this chapter suggests neither its religious base nor its political theory is developed enough, and I regard it as a corrective and supplement to prophetic realism rather than a replacement of it. Chapter 4, "Religion, Morality, and International Politics," develops the deeper connections between religion, morality, and international politics in presenting a philosophy of religion and one of international politics. The danger of absolutizing political judgments under religious influence is discussed under the rubric of "Religious Idealization." Both the complexity and the inevitability of religion and international politics interacting are summarized by "Alan Geyer's Typology," to conclude the chapter.

The fifth chapter, "On Speaking to Hezbollah and a Jewish Settler," is a personal memoir of an attempt at interreligious dialogue that led to a crisis for me and for my church. It led to my receiving death threats, and even a printed editorial by Richard Scaife's newspaper suggesting I should be "stoned" and kicked into the gutter. A national progressive church fired two executives, and threats were received to burn churches with worshippers in them. It reflects the dangers of religious international politics as well as American hesitation to dialogue with enemies of Israel's policies.[3] The second part of the chapter reflects on a dialogue with a Jewish settler on the West Bank and leads to an exploration of Bruggemann's theology of the land and the dangers of religious claims for land. The theme of dialogue is picked up again in the concluding chapter of the book. Who to dialogue with is still a point of contention between administration critics and supporters of American policy in Iraq. Chapter 6 draws upon Moslem historians and others to support a retelling of the situation in religiously divided Iraq under the title of "War and Wisdom from Islam and Christianity."[4] The long history of conflict between Islam and the West is contemporarily complicated by the discussions of *empire* and *democracy*. Both of these concepts are discussed in terms of the philosophy of Reinhold Niebuhr, and the dangers of American attempts to promote both of these militarily in universal terms are analyzed. Chapter 7, "Reflections on Violence and Terrorism," supplements my own understanding of terrorism by drawing upon interviews with terrorists and the writings of the theorists of violence and terrorism. The major interviewers and theorists drawn upon include Fawaz A. Gerges, Marjorie Suchocki,

Vali Nasr, Rene Girard, Robert Hammerton-Kelly, Kristi Sparta, Gil Baille, Mark Jurgensmeyer, Ismael Garcia, Jessica Stern, and Barbara Victor. Religion and terrorism are connected; the precise meaning of these connections is still a subject of debate. The chapter indicates there are deep connections between religious life in the Middle East and terrorism as well as similar connections in Western terrorists. The problem of dealing with terrorism is not simply reforming U.S. policy. There are real dangerous enemies in the world whose immoral attacks on civilians receive support from their religious traditions. These religious connections make the terrorists able to accept martyrdom. In fact as Edward Long, Jr., pointed out, most of the acts of terrorist martyrdom are undertaken by persons grounding their sacrifice in religious convictions.[5] The struggle with religious terrorism is in the long run a struggle with religious support for terrorism and this is in part an ideological struggle and one that has to be won by Moslems within their own societies. Several American Moslem imams have condemned terrorism as non-Islamic,[6] but much more leadership is needed from Moslem leadership in the Middle East. The United States will have to protect itself and fight terrorists even as it is trying to evolve policies that will encourage the fading of religious support for terrorism. Most of the struggles between radical Islamists and other Moslems occur within Moslem societies or in Palestinian attacks upon Israel. Religious differences among Jews prevent Israel politics from acquiring the creative edge it needs to move the peace process forward. The Jewish lobby in the United States prevents America from pushing Israel sufficiently to end the occupation of Palestine on the West Bank and East Jerusalem. Fundamentalist and evangelical preachers in the United States advised both the first and second Presidents Bush regarding going to war in Iraq. Their followers provide the margin of victory for George W. Bush and support unilateral militarism by the administration. Even in the heart of the country the destruction of the Murtha Building by followers of Christian Identity was at first popularly believed to be an attack by Moslems. Critical reflection and reform in religion is one of the changes required to reduce the terrorism threatening the world.

Finally, for these preliminary paragraphs it is important to remember that a crazed fanatical assassination of the Archduke Ferdinand of the Hapsburg Empire and bad responses to that murder ignited World War I, filling the trenches of Europe with four years of the blood of a generation. World War I and its misconceived peace settlement spawned the anti-utopia of the Third Reich and the Holocaust driving the persecuted survivors to the Middle East. Patience and prudence are required to prevent current religious fanaticisms from plunging us into World War III.

Notes

1. Kenneth Vaux, *Ethics and the War on Terrorism* (Eugene: Wipf and Stock Publishers, 2002).

2. Glen Stassen, ed., *Just Peacemaking: Ten Practices for Abolishing War* (Cleveland: Pilgrim Press, 1998).

3. See: John J. Mearsheimer and Stephen M. Walt, *The Israel Lobby and U.S. Foreign Policy* (New York: Farrar, Strauss and Giroux, 2007) for a lengthy analysis of the difficulty of criticizing U.S. foreign policy toward Israel.

4. See: Vali Nasr, *The Shia Revival* (W.W. Norton & Company, 2000) for a sophisticated analysis of the Shia-Sunni struggle rooted in almost 1300 years of religious-political history.

5. Edward Leroy Long, Jr., *Facing Terrorism: Responding as Christians* (Louisville, KY: Westminster John Knox Press, 2004)39.

CHAPTER ONE

~

The Relationship of
Ethics to International Politics

The study of the relationship of international politics to viable ethical traditions is not easy. The subject is complicated by the denseness of both fields. The problem of relating the two is more of a human problem to be lived with than a logical or scientific problem which can be resolved. There are many alternative understandings of international politics, and there are even more different understandings of ethics. The two fields point in different directions. Politics is about the pursuit of self-interest as well as the common good, and international politics is about the pursuit of national purpose or interest and the welfare of the world. Ethics, while recognizing the inevitableness of the pursuit of self-interest, is more concerned about the common good, the right act beyond self-interest, and the appropriateness of one's or a nation's acts in the wider spheres of humanity. Different nations have different goals and needs and there are a variety of ethical systems. Many nations have various of ethical systems within the nation as well as competing understandings of international politics.

The focus of this study is on the military intervention of the United States into the politics of the Middle East. International relations is much more than the study of war and conflict, but when the nations are at war a certain brutality characterizes international relations. It is not enough to utter with General Sherman, "War is hell," and to act as if there is no judgment whether divine or human. General Sherman's war had conflicting purposes: the retention or not of slavery and the preservation or dismemberment of the Union. There were rules even for this most terrible of wars for United States' citizens; sometimes they were honored and sometimes they were set aside. Both armies and both commanders believed deeply that God's providential rule was being expressed through the slaughter. The history of political theory is full of this ambiguity and there are a variety of solutions to the relationship of morals to international politics and war.[1]

The *New Testament* assumes there will be wars until the end of time and this conviction is attributed to Jesus, himself a victim of military execution by an occupying power in the mix of Middle Eastern religious and political struggle. Yet he is solemnly regarded as teaching a profound way of peace and of blessing the peacemakers. His ethics are a mixture of the most extreme demands, but also of a practical suggestion about negotiations when one is outnumbered.

Thucydides' *The Peloponnesian War* presents a humanistic interpretation of war, breaking with Homer's sense that war was the gods' manipulation of human fates. War here grows out of human conflicts and inadequate diplomacy in power-seeking city-states. Realist texts often quote the utterance of his portrayal of the Athenian General before slaughtering the Melians: "The strong do what they have the power to do and the weak accept what they have to accept." Yet is not our story regarding American power in Iraq more complicated? It would seem the strong do what they have the power to do, but that often they are limited by moral norms or that moral understandings become the basis of critique of what the strong (e.g., prison guards) have done because they had the power.

Augustine in the *City of God* knew that conflicts would rage in the City of Earth until the end of time; he also knew personally as a bishop how conflict tore apart the City of God. Following Plato and Cicero, he thought there were standards by which a nation could decide about the justice of entering a conflict. Armed forces were necessary in North Africa, but not everything men would do in war was justifiable. He divided the ethic of perfection for the monks and the church from the rougher ethics needed to defend the City of Earth. Thomas Aquinas, having abandoned his military role, would systematize Augustine's insights and form the basis of the impressive tradition of just war teaching based on natural law for Roman Catholic civilization.

Machiavelli in the sixteenth century of competing city-states in Italy found it more important to appear to be religiously righteous and moral than actually to be so. Rulers were advised to do what was necessary to survive as rulers rather than to seek moral goodness. Self-seeking of power under the guise of religion continues to be a perennial issue in the politics of nations. His advice in *The Prince* still survives in American colleges as the text for the instruction in the *real politick* many instructors assume the students need to know to manage the American republic or empire. His *Institutes* provide a more complete vision which guided his politics as a statesman in the Florentine Republic seeking the unity of Italy, though even here his vision is amoral.

His contemporary, John Calvin, guided his city-state more successfully than Machiavelli with as realistic a vision of human nature. But Calvin's politics were characterized by a much higher place for rules grounded in religion as a regulating and limiting force than Machiavelli. Calvin becomes a symbol of legalism on realist grounds while Machiavelli remains as a symbol of immorality on realist grounds.

Thomas Hobbes said his mother gave birth to fear and himself on the news of the Spanish Armada's projected invasion in 1588. His theology is recognizably in debt to John Calvin, but he places the sovereign beyond the moral critique of the people. Sovereignty was all that could save the people from their anarchical "War of all against all." Political philosophers respecting the idea of social contract have founded both idealism and realism upon Hobbes' myth. However, everyone can recognize how the lack of sovereignty gives a tendency toward anarchy in the international system. Too often Americans have thought that the solution to international political wars was a world government or sovereign. They have been able to suggest this only by ignoring the de Tocqueville insight that the American constitution is founded upon a common history, economy, religion, and foe against whom they had just rebelled.

The ambiguity of morality in international politics in times of conflict is referenced in the conversation between Stalin and Churchill in which Stalin suggested executing the top 50,000 officers in the German army. Churchill rejected the idea on the grounds of morality and British honor. Of course, historically hundreds of thousands of German prisoners in Russian captivity were permitted to starve, die from disease, freeze to death, or were otherwise killed. Less than a tenth of the prisoners from the Battle of Stalingrad ever returned to Germany. The British terror bombing of Germany cities, though understandable as the one tactic the British had to inflict harm on Germany at one stage of the war, is only marginally less morally repugnant than the killing of prisoners.

Postwar American experience runs from John Foster Dulles' denunciation of his allies invasion of Egypt in 1956 in moral terms to Robert Kennedy's refusal to sanction an air attack on Cuba during the missile crisis because he said it would be morally wrong, as was the surprise attack on Pearl Harbor. Both John Foster Dulles and Robert Kennedy combined realism and morality in politics. Both could sound very idealistic and act very realistic. Dulles' displayed his idealism particularly before becoming Secretary of State when he led the Federal Council of Churches in a very successful program and attempt to strengthen the drive toward the international organization of the United Nations. The idealism broke out again against his allies in the Suez invasion and in his rhetoric regarding strengthening the United Nations in which he believed so deeply. Robert Kennedy, often regarded as cynical, displayed his sense of morality in the missile crisis over Cuba, but his tactics were Machiavellian in the attempts on Castro's life and the alliance with the mafia. Finally his run for the Presidency in 1968 was couched in terms of American idealism even if aspects of the campaign seemed to descend into the rougher aspects of the realities of electoral politics in America.

The attempt at moral reasoning about the crisis in the Middle East during President G.W. Bush's terms enters into this ambiguous terrain. To what extent do the conflicts with actors in the region justify the setting aside of moral restraints? Can a sophisticated approach to moral reflection on international politics guide U.S. foreign policy in a wise manner which serves both the long range purposes of the United States and the moral sensibilities of a significant portion of the American people? It is widely recognized that moral philosophy or ethics can be undertaken without specific reference to religion, but in fact religious resources are the great generators of moral reflection in the United States. This is also true of Islamic civilization where religion plays a decisive role in politics. This study in international politics focused on the Middle East also takes very seriously the religious aspirations of the actors and the relationship of their religious confessions to ethics and politics. The author, of course, has his own combination of moral and religious perspectives on the international politics of the United States which he addresses as prophetic or moral realism. Throughout the study the differences between this perspective and others will be resolved by argument and not by confession. This is to say that the controlling perspective is that of philosophy which adjudicates with reason and evidence between different perspectives on religion, morals, and international politics. So the book while grounded in a particular approach or school of thought is a philosophy of morals, politics, and religion.

Three Philosophers of International Politics and a Typology of Morals

H. Richard Niebuhr noted in his posthumously published volume, *The Responsible Self,*[2] the emergence of the moral meaning of the term *responsibility*. The rise of the term as a primary category for human self-understanding is rooted, he thought, in certain characteristics of our general knowledge of humanity in the twentieth century. The word *responsibility* is supplanting the words *duty, good, law, virtue,* and *morality* in moral discourse and this replacement is not merely a shift in vocabulary. Rather, the symbol of responsibility links contemporary patterns of meaning and current notions of motivation in a general mode of the meaning of moral action today.

Niebuhr's attempt in this book is to analyze moral discourse and to discover the patterns of human moral life. There may be more prescription in his study than he confesses. He is convincingly arguing for the adoption of a model and not simply noting that it has arrived. He believes that human behavior exhibits the quality of responsiveness as he describes it, but he also knows that he is attempting to displace the other two models of human moral life from their claims to primary recognition.

A symbol that has proven very fruitful in the past is humanity as the maker of artifacts and concepts. The model of humanity as artist, technician, or fashioner has been adapted to the moral life. Aristotle began his *Ethics*, "Every art and every inquiry and similarly every action and pursuit is thought to aim at some good." Humanity acts toward ends and human beings act to fashion themselves toward a goal or an end.

In the light of this model humanity acts purposively to mold ends and in so doing they shape themselves as makers.

This image of "Humanity the maker" supports all ethical theories regarded as teleological, that is, theories which determine what ought to be done by reference to the goal or *telos* being desired. There is a degree of necessity for this type of thinking. H. Richard Niebuhr wrote:

> When we are dealing with this human nature of ours, in ourselves and in others, as administrators of our private realms of body and mind or as directors of social enterprises—from families seeking happiness to international societies seeking peace—we cannot fail to ask: "At what long—or short—range state of affairs are we aiming, and what are the immediate steps that must be taken toward the attainment of the possible goal?"

People who have used this image have not agreed upon the best ends to be pursued. They have disagreed on means to be utilized even when agreeing on goals. They have exhibited wide disagreement as to what the human nature was which was to be shaped. These disagreements, however, have reflected some agreement on the nature of personal existence. Humanity makes itself and its environment in light of chosen goals.

A second dominant model of the moral life has been that of humanity as citizen. Life, in this view, is not art—for human nature is not clay to be molded. The human body, sentiments, and passions are more like citizens to be ruled than clay to be molded. Humanity the maker can reject inadequate material, but we have been given our selves and our communities with their histories. H. Richard Niebuhr raises the question: "What use would it have been had Socrates designed for himself that happy life which Aristotle described." We cannot select our destiny; the most we can do is decide by which rules we will rule ourselves. Life is more like politics, the art of the possible, than like the architecture of designing and constructing a cathedral. Humans are confronted with prescriptions, rules, mores, laws, and the influence of societal pressures. We can only ask to what laws will we assent and against which laws will we rebel.

Contemporary religion across this country relates itself very closely to this model of the moral life. The church understands itself in thousands of places as the guardian of the moral law. The moral law is seen as revealed by God and is often compared in popular pulpit rhetoric to the law of nature. As the law of gravity forces objects to return to earth and is ignored only at great peril, so the moral law is seen as a guard against destruction. Campaigns to keep the Ten Commandments on public buildings reflect this understanding as do the bracelets asking "What would Jesus do?" Church practices denouncing perceived violators of the moral law reflect this law sense of morality. The failure to discern and to discuss by what models of morality a perceived violator might be acting are often engendered by a simple understanding of rule or law morality. However, there are antinomian tendencies in American society which undermine widely perceived understandings of morality. Rules are needed, but so are perceptions of their evolution and their relativity.

To a considerable degree, Christianity is bound to this model as long as it holds to its scriptures. Matthew viewed Jesus as the eschatological giver of the laws to those receiving grace. Paul wrestled with the issues of conflicting laws throughout his life. The basic human dilemma for much of orthodox Protestantism is how can rebellious humanity, which has from the Garden of Eden violated the law and the covenants, be saved from the wrath of a righteous God? The human story from Genesis through Romans is seen through a model of jurisprudence with the image of humanity as the unworthy citizen of God's Kingdom as a dominating motif.

The primordial nature of the mythology of humanity as law abider is witnessed to in the myths of origin of Greek and Mesopotamian culture. The cosmos reflects the ordering of the human world and the gods who direct the cosmos also direct humanity. The model has illuminated human moral experience in primitive and contemporary culture. Tyranny and democracy both shape their community's life by appeals to law and order. It has helped in making complex decisions, and the roles of both Solon and Kant in the cultural experience of the Western world give evidence of its power. The role of law as a model in determining morality in Islam seems stronger than in the Western world. The West's flexibility about some of the law tradition is seen in Islam as a reason for antagonism toward the West, but also as a desired liberation for some modern Moslems. Even within Islam, the Shia interpretation of law has been more flexible than the Sunni tradition historically, though Khommeni's Shia regime enforced the law more in accordance with a strict Sunni tendency.

Debates between the representatives of the teleological school (makers) and deontological school (citizens) have not been conclusive. For those who focus on ends, rules are utilitarian in character; they are guides to the end. The rule-oriented person can insist, however, that only the life lived according to right standards is good. The moral life is not to be suspended for some future end. The end probably will not be unambiguously achieved anyway. The right life is demanded in the present. Both Islamic groups and Western nations have tended to set aside rules of which they are aware under the emergency conditions of the struggle between American and al Qaeda. There are strong deontological tendencies both in the Old Testament and in the Koran. However, philosophers from Immanuel Kant to R.M. Hare also represent this tradition. Yet the newness of situations in social struggles drives many toward utilitarian arguments which are hard to refute in societal issues. Issues of civil disobedience or revolution often drive toward pragmatic or utilitarian forms of argument, though they can be analyzed in deontological terms as well with relevant rules for the conflicts.

American philosophers have summarized the debate in ways that tend to produce a synthesis. Both terms of *right* and *good* can be regarded as fundamental in moral philosophy, and it is recognized that anyone who works long with one term may find oneself in need of the other. C. H. Broad has called those who attempt to use both terms and methods as Federalists. H. R. Niebuhr is critical of those who go to a double theory without the parts being adequately harmonized. Those images are helpful, but they are only hypotheses, not copies of the reality of the moral life. Something rests, he believes, beyond the limits of the adequacy of these images.

The inadequacies of the previous images permitted H. R. Niebuhr to consider the emerging model of humanity as the answerer. This is the implied image behind the emphasis upon responsibility. A person is engaged in dialogue with other selves and one forms oneself by responding to other selves and by reacting to their perceptions. Humanity exists in reaction to stimuli. Even history is being written not so much in terms of ideals or laws, but in terms of societal responses to challenges in the environment, he contends. The understanding of humanity as responsive beings who answer to action upon themselves with acts in accordance with their interpretation of the action illuminates aspects of conduct that the previous emphasis upon citizen or maker obscured. The model is not completely new; aspects of it are found in Greek philosophy, and E. Clinton Gardner showed how helpful the model was in illuminating biblical ethics in his widely used text *Biblical Faith and Social Ethics*.³ Women students of ethics have often found this model more illuminating of their moral experience than the other models.

Practical life also reflects the pattern of responsive action in testing and breaking of societies and persons. Suffering social or personal calls forth a response which shapes the ethos of the community and the character of the individual. Ideals, goals, and laws play a role in shaping a country's response to emergency, but the response in action itself shapes the life and self-definition of the community. The hatred and fanaticism engendered in the Islamic community by the United States' response to 9/11 shapes people in those communities. The invasion of Iraq, in addition to the fatalities inflicted on Iraq and coalition soldiers, is returning to the United States veterans, 35 percent of whom need, according to the Department of Defense report, mental health therapy. Similarly immigrants to the United States are experiencing more difficulty in obtaining public health benefits and other services since the war began. The action of the war itself, as the Vietnam War before it, influences the ethos and meaning of the people of the United States.

Using the terms of value, the difference between the three perceptions of moral actions might be described as the *good*, the *right*, and the *fitting*. The ethical question is not simply: "What is my end?" or "What is my duty?", but rather first: "What is going on?" The fitting action, the one that fits the total interaction as response and anticipation of further response is the only action which could contribute maximally to the good and is only action which can be said to be right. Niebuhr defines his understanding of responsibility as an image of the moral life:

> The idea or pattern of responsibility, then, may summarily and abstractly be defined as the idea of an agent's action as response to an action upon him in accordance with his interpretation of the latter action and with his expectation of response to his response; all of this in a continuous community of agents.

Three Philosophers of Statecraft

The usefulness of the typology can be tested by the outlines of the moral theory of three figures of influence in recent U.S. foreign policy discussions to see how their moral theories of the conduct of foreign policy reflect the types of humanity as citizen, maker, or responder. Somewhat arbitrarily, the discussion will focus on three all of whom had influence in circles of both Christian ethics and government. They include a leading churchman and Secretary of State, John Foster Dulles, the most important theorist of international politics who was informed by Judaism, Hans J. Morgenthau, and a theologian and potential Secretary of State, Reinhold Niebuhr.

Though his specific judgments as to what morality demanded varied from time to time, Dulles was certain of the importance of morality in international politics. Moving with the rigor of a Calvinist, he had few of the reservations about the limits of morality in international politics which characterized the more Lutheran Reinhold Niebuhr.

As Chairman of the Federal Council of Churches Commission to Study the Bases of a Just and Durable Peace, Dulles hammered his own philosophy of international morality into the churches' official thinking. The Commission's early stage was dominated by the question of moral principle. The Commission's *Statement of Guiding Principles*,[4] which Dulles had drafted, was approved by the Delaware National Study conference. These thirteen principles served as the formal foundation for the work of the Commission. The *Principles* included recognition that God, revealed in Jesus Christ, is the author of the moral law. This moral law undergirds the world and the recent troubles of the world (World War II) are a result of disregarding the moral law. The moral law demands cooperation and mutual concern; revenge and retaliation are contrary to the law. The *Principles* called for international machinery to regulate economics, armaments, colonies, to promote change in treaties, and to ensure the basic freedoms in keeping with the moral order. Special responsibilities rested with the United States and the church in building world community. Christian citizens were called upon by the *Principles* to seek to "translate their beliefs into practical realities and to create a public opinion which will insure that the United States shall play its full and essential part in the creation of a moral way of international living."[5]

Six of the thirteen principles explicitly referred to the moral law. The others implicitly suggested the primacy of this moral law. The Commission throughout its life in the 1940s stressed the importance of the moral law, which was the equivalent of natural law. The moral law in the first principle is regarded as analogous to the physical law. In the final principle it is recognized that for Christians God is the author of this moral law. The content of the moral law was not explicated in the *Principles*, but the affirmation of the moral law did serve to give authority to the internationalist trend of the *Principles*.

During the life of the Commission, Dulles made clear his views of Jesus' ethical teaching. Jesus had taught to subordinate the material things and to utilize fully the spiritual powers. His teaching was not directed to a particular social situation, or to a trans-historical Kingdom of God, but to people throughout the ages. He formulated principles which people could follow in changing human situations. Dulles reflected the teachings of the synoptic gospels, read with a lawyer's mind, reflecting his own situation in mid-twentieth-century America. Dulles' writing reveals little acquaintance with Paul and less with the disciplines of theology or biblical scholarship. This is a little extraordinary as his father was a professor of theology and he himself served on the board of directors of Union Theological Seminary. He argued that the roots of the mission of the American people are found in Jesus' teaching. Christ wanted people to see and think clearly, to have compassion, and to act. Recapturing the qualities that Jesus taught would provide the moral dynamic needed to win both the war and the peace. "The broad principles that should govern our international conduct are not obscure. They grow out of the practice by the nations of the simple things Christ taught."

As Secretary of State in the Dwight Eisenhower administration he found himself locked in the Cold War struggle with the Soviet Union. He expedited the conclusion of the Korean War by threatening to use nuclear weapons, articulated the concept of "roll back" for Soviet power, opposed colonization and the British–French expedition to retake the Suez Canal in 1956, and tended to rely on nuclear deterrence to contain the Soviet Union. His language was bellicose and legalistic, but with the exception of the intervention to overthrow socialist regimes in Guatemala and Iran he and Eisenhower kept the United States out of war. It could be argued that their stubbornness about Vietnam and their aid to the French laid the grounds for the disaster of the Vietnam War, but their investment there was small and could have been abandoned by John F. Kennedy during his years as president. The massive war by the United States in Vietnam was really the fault of the Johnson administration, and of President Richard Nixon's continuation of it. The Cold War obscured the teaching of the churchman, but the tendency toward legalism and reliance on the United Nations for which the Commission had campaigned still endured. Late in his career as Secretary of State, Dulles articulated his position in words which reveal the continuity of his philosophy. He spoke before a group of church leaders who were maintaining Dulles' earlier position that the government in Peking was the real government of China and that it should be admitted to the United Nations.

> I assure you that President Eisenhower and his Secretary of State accept it that, as put in the first Guiding Principle, "There is a moral order which is fundamental and eternal, and which is relevant to corporate life of men and the ordering of human society." We seek conscientiously to act in accordance with that concept.

Realism

Hans J. Morgenthau dominated thinking about international politics after the publication of his major work *Politics Among Nations: The Struggle for Power and Peace*. Though his philosophy of international politics evolved, he is known for his political realism and for a book In *Defense of the National Interest*[6] that in reaction to what he regarded as moralism he articulated a hard politics relating ethics very close to national interest. He even suggested that moral principles could be derived from political reality. Some have treated him as a modern Machiavellian, though this is far from helpful in describing Morgenthau. He saw the clash between ethics and politics while appreciating how moral guidelines could limit the drive of nations to maximize their power. Morality could close some alternatives as in Churchill's refusal to execute Germany officers. He tended to regard politics as evil as it consisted of influencing to control other people, but that ethics could lead states people to choose the lesser evil in a fallen world. He protested against utilitarianism in morality and revealed a Kantian rule ethic mentality in many of his judgments. He did not have the sense that Dulles had that ethics could encourage politicians to pursue moral ends, but he saw that ethical principles informed the political actors they were acting badly and in some cases politicians would act less badly under moral critique. In his first book in English, *Scientific Man vs. Power Politics*, he wrote:

> Political ethics is indeed the ethics of doing evil. . . . Its last resort, then is the endeavor to choose, since evil there must be, among several possible actions the one that is the least evil.[7]

Later in his campaigning to save Soviet Judaism and in *The Purpose of American Politics* his moral passions led him to more positive statements. He is remembered besides being a great political theorist, though, for his pessimism about what was possible in politics, and for an ethic of principles which criticized rather than drove foreign policy. In terms of the typology of morality suggested, he belongs to the humanity-as-citizen type under duty with a movement toward the humanity-as-answerer position.

Reinhold Niebuhr, a potential Secretary of State, in an Adalai Stevenson administration, approached the ethics of international politics in a manner very close to his brother's model of humanity as answerer. He was a Christian pragmatist or moral realist whom I have elsewhere described as a Prophetic Realist. There is a residual loyalty to a morality of rules in a confessed tradition that prevents Reinhold from easily moving into his brother's category in personal morality, but in social morality his writing fits the model.

His emphasis since the early days of World War II was that as the illusions of U.S. innocence and isolation were shattered, the United States had to assume responsibility on the international scene while avoiding the dangers of imperialism. There were no eternal ends in international politics; he had none of Dulles' confidence that a just and stable order could be created. Guiding rules or regulative principles could be tentatively articulated as long as the historical contingencies of their forms were recognized. Fundamentally, however, a nation needs to understand itself—its greatness and its weakness—and attempt to respond to the terrors of the international scene while securing as best it can the interests of its own people generously conceived with the other nations in mind. He was close to Morgenthau in his critique of Dulles' moralism, and while John Foster Dulles would complain in private about Niebuhr being so critical of him, he did not do so publicly.

All three of our philosophers are in some sense Federalists in moral theory as they to some degree mix deontology and teleological judgments. All three to a degree are aware that in the political realm ethical-political decisions have elements of response in them. However, in their formal writing on ethics and politics they reveal distinct differences.

None of the three represent H. Richard Niebuhr's pure types, nor would he have expected them to correspond exactly. Thinkers can only rarely be correlated precisely with any typology. Many other factors than morality impinge on policy and it is difficult to abstract an actor's moral preference from policy recommendation. Morgenthau exhibits a certain tension between his writing on politics and his writing on ethics and politics that exposes certain unresolved issues in his thought. Roger Shinn has discussed this tension as indicative of a Lutheran if not quite a Manichean dualism and summarized his position, "In Morgenthau we see the paradox of the realist and the moralist."[8]

If the typology is presented on a spectrum with the left side represented by deontology and the right by a response ethic, the thinkers may be arranged from left to right as: John Foster Dulles, Hans J. Morgenthau, and Reinhold Niebuhr. Dulles combines deontology with teleology in the ethics of foreign policy. Morgenthau combines a rule morality with a certain tendency toward a response ethic. The rule ethic which seems primary often forces him to doubt the possibility of a viable morality of international affair. The rules reveal the immorality. In practice he is more a responder like Reinhold Niebuhr, but in ethical theory he is more of a formalist. Also he has a residual hope for a world government which Reinhold Niebuhr does not share. Reinhold Niebuhr's post–World War II thought on moral issues in international affairs fits his brother's pattern of a responsive ethic very well. His ethic contains the elements of a very weak deontology which are part of a response ethic as worked out by H. Richard Niebuhr as the regulative principles or guidelines which nations need to live in community. The elements of regulating morality by long-range ends in the sense of creating an ordered world to fit a prescribed goal are very few. Some means are still justified by the ends being pursued in the context of responsive action in an historical situation, but it is not a teleological ethic as presented in the typology. He is somewhat less teleological than Morgenthau and radically less so than Dulles. His thought more easily bridges the gap between ethics and politics than does Morgenthau's philosophy. He is also more active in practical politics than Morgenthau and less so than John Foster Dulles. He has criticized Morgenthau for divorcing love too absolutely from power in *Man's Nature and His Communities*,[9] and for conceding too much ground to the perfectionist versions of Christianity in the debate over ethics and politics in *Reinhold Niebuhr: a Prophetic Voice in Our Time*.[10]

Summary

John Foster Dulles' ethics and politics are integrated, and this integration is seen in his understanding of rules of international conduct and his plans for world order. He moves as an intra-mundane ascetic in Max Weber's terms to reform the world. His Calvinism first expressed in his campaign for the United Nations development and then in the Peace Treaty with Japan got expressed in his militant rhetoric vis-à-vis the Soviet Union in the Cold War. But even here distinctions must be made between the rhetoric of the Calvinist lawyer and the peace he helped maintain as Secretary of State.

Hans J. Morgenthau's politics and ethics are in different realms. The political actor is always tempted to use morality as ideological cover for the pursuit of his interests. Morality properly conceived reveals the fundamental immorality of international politics. The only relevant ethic is a prudential one which honors the relevant ethical principles and applies them circumspectly. His early writing distanced morality from ethics more widely than his later ones which found moral purpose in the American experiment to maintain principles of equality and freedom. His latest writings also found resources in the religious life of Lincoln and in his own Judaism which he honored.

In international politics Reinhold Niebuhr recommends a contextual, pragmatic ethic which considers the interests of other nations while pursuing and securing the interests of one's own country. Morality is defined in terms of responsibility to protect values, maintain some order, and critique a nation's pretensions. Plans for world order are largely illusory and the conduct of international affairs is often characterized by hypocrisy.

Writing mostly during World War II and the Cold War, his writings stress the worthiness of defending the American experiment and values, and are highly contextual and relative to the situation. His skill at critique of the nation's lack of justice, his understanding of the dangers to the nation, and his hopes for national renewal all grounded in his own synthesis of the meaning of Biblical religion have led several interpreters to refer to him as a prophetic figure.

What is Going On?

The third type of moral decision making presented by H. Richard Niebuhr suggested that the crucial question is: "What is going on?" Let's assume that question about current approaches to U.S. foreign policy, but place the policy question in a larger framework. Michael Doyle's important work[11] on theory of international politics admittedly prefers realist models of theory, but he suggests that there are three major types. A recent approach developed by Robert Keohane drawing upon Immanuel Kant and the evolution of international organizations has been labeled Institutional Theory. It corrects realist theory by noting how important international institutions have become since World War II. The world is woven together by understandings regarding communication, laws of the seas, international law as it develops, and important institutions like the World Bank, The International Monetary Fund, the United Nations, the World Trade Organizations, the World Court, the emerging International Criminal Court, North Atlantic Treaty Alliance, the European Union, dozens of trade agreements, human rights agreements, and thousands of international organizations across borders. John Foster Dulles' emphasis upon moral principle, the United Nations, and the role of the church are early forerunners of this recognition as was Woodrow Wilson's passion for the League of Nations. Kant's early theory also stressed the role of commerce in unifying the world and making war too economically inefficient to have a future. He also stressed the role of democratic institutions in lessening the propensity of nations to enter war. A body of recent theory has also developed the idea that democracies do not fight each other. The democratic peace theory has also recognized that democratic nations may make war on non-democratic countries frequently as the United States has been very warlike in its history.

A second form of theory recognized by Doyle, he calls Liberation Theory. This body of thought does not adjust to the international system as much as it tries to change it. The Liberation analyses of theology proposed changing the system particularly as it related to Latin America. Marxist theories found the root of international conflict in imperialistic capitalism and believed it was necessary to overthrow capitalism to achieve justice and peace. Some radical Islamists seem to believe that throwing the United States and Israel out of the Middle East would promote peace and stability in the region. Critics of empire like Michael Hardt, in *Empire*, often see the overthrow of imperialism as the key to prosperity and peace. There is also the militant democratic program pushed by neoconservative thinkers to promote peace by democratizing as much of the world as possible. This liberationist perspective is fueled by the democratic peace thesis on the one hand and by the promotion of laissez-faire economics on the other. This program has been supported by a worldwide system of developing military capacity to assure victory in any conflict the United States is engaged in and to support vital U.S. interests anywhere in the world. From different points of origin, Donald Rumsfeld, Richard Cheney, Condoleezza Rice, George W. Bush, Paul Wolfewitz, and major actors of the Bush administration and their supporters in various research organizations have been brought to this perspective which is being challenged and tested in the Middle East currently. The Liberationists disagree about many things, but their basic commonality is the commitment to changing the system through radical measures.

The third perspective noted is that of various kinds of realism, grounded in the thought of Augustine, Calvin, Hobbes, recently Reinhold Niebuhr, Hans J. Morgenthau, and carried forward today by Kenneth Waltz, John Merscheimer, Rober Kagan, Henry Kissinger, and a host of others. In the debates about policy in Washington this view is attributed to long-term professionals in the State Department who have not shared the Defense Department's enthusiasm for the Iraq invasion. This group knows that the world changes, but is hesitant to risk a great deal in the thought that one country can change it very much. They tend to be incrementalists. Some rest their conclusions in deep moral philosophies, and some refuse to do so, being more impressed with Machiavelli than are moral realists. Currently the realists are more inclined to insist on more diplomacy and multilateral approaches while the neoconservative promoters of democracy feel that the U.S. dominance in military matters gives it a unique opportunity to make the world better and less dangerous for the United States

While the argument above distinguished moral realism from neoconservative models of statecraft the neoconservative argument has greater strengths than presented so far. The neoconservative institutions and thinkers have prided themselves on having better ideas than their liberal critics, and they have brushed aside some of the limits that the liberal institutionalists have favored. The relegating of the United Nations to a relatively insignificant role in security issues is one example. The neoconservative movement has benefited from the democratic peace thesis, and is able to argue democratic institutions in several Middle Eastern states might make the region more peaceful and possibly also more prosperous or at least more democratic in sharing its wealth than it has been to date. The President argues that democratic countries will not harbor terrorists, though the evidence for that thesis is weaker than the peace thesis. But the neoconservative view seems strong because it has taken pieces from the institutionalist approach and joined them to the old power politics. It smacks of the idealism of the American republic as voiced by the idealism of both Woodrow Wilson and John Foster Dulles. The realists tend to note that both these idealists were sons of Calvinist manses, and probably trusted too much in the power of preached ideals. All of this joins with a desire to see the United States succeed in a period when its security has been threatened by terrorism. At the popular level the joining of the above analysis to popular folk religion, which tends to religiously legitimate the role of the United States as a superpower, provides support for an adventuresome war in the Middle East. Additionally, the war in the middle of the Middle East if successful, or perhaps even if not, takes pressure off of Israel by destroying the only threatening army in the Middle East to Israel, that of Iraq. The strengthening of Israel is seen for religious and political reasons as a blessing to both some Jews and Christian Zionists giving even more support to the neoconservative arguments. It must be noted also that leading realist theoreticians like Hans J. Morgenthau and Reinhold Niebuhr both supported Zionism in their day.

Another consideration is why do nations go to war anyway? I have argued elsewhere that the prophets, particularly Isaiah, understood that war took place because there was no sovereign power to prevent it, because there was no agreed-upon moral standards among the nations, because people were prideful and greedy, and because the rich oppressed the poor. Kenneth Waltz in an earlier book *Man, State, and War*[12] argued that the three main reasons that philosophers gave for war breaking out were due to fallen human nature, misshaped states, and international anarchy. Political realism emphasizes all three reasons as explanatory for the willingness of states to risk the dangers of war. Waltz's early study may not have given enough weight to the ideological reasons for going to war, I think the prophet Isaiah covered this when he spoke of the haughtiness of the rulers and their not knowing what they should have known. None of this realistic analysis argues that any particular war is inevitable, though realism does expect wars between nations as long as we are in this historical epoch, organized around relatively autonomous nation states, even when they are becoming more interdependent. Peace is not the only value for the realists seeking to guide foreign policy, but it is a very high value. This is especially true because at times of war other values are under great risk. A great achievement of the twentieth century was the avoidance of a major war between the Soviet Union and the United States. Their were proxy wars throughout the Cold War, and the United States intervened in Russia attempting to prevent the Communist victory at the end of World War I, but the major cataclysm was avoided until time eroded the causes for the struggle. Argentina and Chile avoided war at the tip of South America through papal arbitration. Many conflicts have been avoided, and even after armed struggle nations find they still need to negotiate, though sometimes under a rearranged balance of power.

Of course, the answer to: "What is going on?" is relative to whomever is arguing about the meaning of a particular struggle, but one issue is the debate between the traditional, realist reluctance to extend the United States into difficult conflicts on the Asian mainland and the neoconservative perspective enriched with American idealism and religious consciousness of a particular kind that is eager to remold the Middle East. Put in terms of the earlier discussion of morality the neoconservative aggression is teleological or goal oriented, while the realist perspective is less sure of far-reaching goals and worries about what is appropriate action. In terms of the political theory presented by Doyle it is a debate between a predominantly moral, realistic perspective and a liberationist perspective. The administration wants to liberate Iraq while the realists would be happy to contain Iraq from threatening vital U.S. interests. In terms of the moral theory presented by H. Richard Niebuhr it is a debate between optimistic teleologists and more pessimistic responders. Both schools have concerns about the rules of war, and because these are a major contribution of ethics to international religious thought we will turn toward the rules of war in the next chapter.

Notes

1. A more expanded form of the discussion of political philosophers of realism is found in Ronald. H. Stone, *Prophetic Realism: Beyond Militarism and Pacifism in an Age of Terror* (New York: T & T Clark, 2005) 10–26.

2. H. Richard Niebuhr, *The Responsible Self* (New York: Harper & Row Publishers, 1963). I heard a form of these lectures at Riverside Church in New York City in the winter of 1962. The lectures were cut short by his illness. Of the various texts I chose for my first full course in Christian ethics at Vassar College this book was the most welcomed by the women students there. This theme of responsibility as an overarching motif for moral reflection appeared in the later years of H. Richard Niebuhr's

teaching according to his son, Richard Niebuhr, who edited the volume from his Glasgow lectures of 1960. Reinhold Niebuhr told me in 1968, that he felt his brother, Helmut and he were at their closest in their formal work in ethics in this volume. Direct quotes are from pages 50, 60, 65.

3. E. Clinton Garner, one of H. Richard Niebuhr's students, wrote the heavily used text book *Biblical Faith in Social Ethics* (New York: Harper & Brothers, 1960) as an introduction to Christian ethics text, but it also demonstrated the deep Biblical roots of H. R. Niebuhr's Christian philosophy in *The Responsible Self*.

4. The Commission to Study the Bases of a Just and Durable Peace of the Federal Council of Churches of Christ in America, *A Just and Durable Peace*. 1941.

5. *Principles and Policies in a Changing World*, Department of State Press Release, No. 701 (Washington, Nov. 18, 1958) 1.

6. Hans J. Morgenthau, *In Defense of the National Interest* (Alfred A. Knopf, 1951)33.

7. Hans J. Morgenthau, *Scientific Man vs. Power Politics* (Chicago: University of Chicago Press, 1946)202.

8. Roger L. Shinn, "Hans Morgenthau: Realist and Moralist," *Worldview*, XIII (January, 1970)10.

9. Reinhold Niebuhr, *Man's Nature and His Communities* (New York: Charles Scribner's Sons, 1965)75-76.

10. Harold L. Landon, ed., *Reinhold Niebuhr: A Prophetic Voice in Our Time* (Greenwich: The Seabury Press, 1962).

11. Michael W. Doyle, *Ways of War and Peace* (New York: W. W. Norton, 1997).

12. Kenneth N. Waltz, *Man, the State, and War: A Theoretical Analysis* (New York: Columbia University Press, 1959).

CHAPTER TWO

~

Just War and Jihad

Moral thinking has tried to place limits on war, and sometimes this thought has had effects. The major product of this thinking has been the justifiable war theory. Because the results of war are dead people and things broken, it has been recognized that such a widespread calamity has needed justification. For reasons discussed in the previous chapter, it seems that modern humanity has evolved into a very war-oriented species. The husband and wife team of the Durants argued that in the last 3,421 years only 268 years had been without war. The study was in 1968 and there have been wars every year since the study. The concept of a just war was present in Plato from whom Cicero took it. Ambrose, who was a general before becoming bishop, learned of it from Cicero and Augustine from Ambrose. Since Augustine the vast majority of Christian theologians have regarded it as possible to morally justify a war under certain conditions. Augustine had no love for war; he regarded it sorrowfully and thought that Christians could enter into war only regretfully. Medieval jurisprudence developed the concept beyond Augustine's few sentences about it, and Thomas Aquinas put three principles of justified war more clearly than Augustine from whom he drew them. A significant minority of Christian theologians have dissented from this development and witnessed to a variety of arguments for pacifism. Technological developments in weapons have in the modern period threatened to render the justifiable war tradition obsolete. But just war thinkers have responded: "You cannot repeal just war teaching, you can only violate it." The tendency of modern warfare to be raged against civilians—whether by carpet bombing or guerrilla warfare—is from the justifiable war perspective morally wrong as it violates the very principles by which a conflict could be justified. Justifiable war thinking is not a casuistic way of justifying what otherwise cannot be justified, but it a rule based way of thinking as to whether or not a conflict can be justified.

Just war theory is taught both in seminaries and military academies and represents one of the meeting places of ethics and international politics. The standards of just war theory are not all exactly the same, but there is a rough consensus as to the outlines of the rules or principles. Arthur Holmes' anthology *War and Christian Ethics*[1] presents a summary list of the principles: *Just cause*; *Just intent*; *Last resort*; *Lawful declaration*; *Limited objectives*; and *Limited means*. Others that show up regularly in the lists of principles are *proportionality* and *success*. Paul Ramsey interpreted Augustine forty-five years ago to ground the need for justifiable war in the need to defend those who could not defend themselves. It is incumbent on reason to defend people who are under unjustified attack from other people, especially those whose intents were malevolent. The aim of even a justified war is to achieve the conditions of peace. Peace is the goal, but in the world there was the recurrent need to defend one's city or country. Love requires one to feed the hungry and to defend the defenseless. This, of course, means that once the defense is successful, the fighting should end. Justifiable war theory is not an excuse for empire building, but a defensive necessity. The outlines of just war thinking are present in modern armies' manuals of conduct for war regarding the treatment of prisoners, civilians, and so forth.

The United Nations Charter signed by all nations forbids the use of armed force except for defense and then it must be reported to the United Nations for resolution. The Charter does not infringe on the right of defense, but it attempts to provide machinery to resolve the conflicts as soon as possible. Just war theory uses elements of all three models of morality explained in the first chapter. It most clearly is a rule-based ethic derived from reason. It has a goal element, as it following Augustine recognizes the aim of peace even in war. As it requires discussion as to the facts of the case, or to "What is going on?" it has elements of the response ethic. The theory provides guidelines, but how the situation of a particular war fits into or outside of the guidelines is a matter for debate. The Administration of the United States and the churches have disagreed as to the morality of the invasion of Iraq. The General Assembly of the Presbyterian Church, for example, found the war "immoral, illegal, and unwise."

Principles of Just War in Iraq and Afghanistan

Just Cause

The war was undertaken to disarm Iraq of weapons of mass destruction and to break the ties of Iraq to terrorists at war with the United States. Neither cause has been found to be real, and the discrediting of the evidence of Secretary of State Powell before the world contributed to his leaving office. The mistake about weapons has been shifted by the administration to failures of intelligence, but there is widespread belief that the administration contributed pressures to produce intelligence that corresponded to its desire to invade Iraq. Given lack of proof of Iraq ties to the attacks on the United States and the failure to locate existing programs for the developing of weapons of mass destruction, the announced reasons by the United States for the invasion lacked credibility.

After the failure of the previous arguments for the invasion, the government turned to the building of a democracy in Iraq as a reason or cause of the war. The changing of a sovereign nation's form of government has never been seen before as a justified reason for invading another country. The removal of a bad king or a tyrant has been traditionally seen as the responsibility of the people who suffer under the misgovernment and not a cause for a war. If the United States were to intervene in every country suffering under a tyrant, even one who practiced terrorism against his own people, there would be no end to interventions. The justification of a preemptive strike would depend upon clear knowledge of the other country's immediate plans to attack one's own country, and no one who is credible argues that Iraq intended to invade the United States. Iraq was irritating, but one third of its air space was taken over by the United States, and U.N. arms inspectors had access to the country to search for weapons. Iraq—having lost its previous war—was contained, subject to boycotts, and in bad economic shape. It was no threat to the United States. On the other hand, the invasion of Afghanistan can be regarded as serving a just cause. The Taliban government protecting al Qaeda was not recognized as a legitimate government by most countries, and a civil war was in process. The United States supported one side of the civil war to suppress al Qaeda with the support of the United Nations, the Pope, and most of the world community. The United States was seen as in hot pursuit of an enemy who had struck the United States and who would strike again unless suppressed or imprisoned.

Just Intent

The requirement of the just intent is similar to the just cause. The intent must be peace and war is not to be undertaken for economic gain or territorial expansion. The whole Persian Gulf area has been declared a vital interest by the U.S. government. That is because of the supply of oil. The first Gulf War was to prevent Iraq from seizing the oil production of Kuwait or maybe of Saudi Arabia. If the war were intended to ensure control of oil resources or to secure long-term U.S. military bases the intent would not have been just. Given the U.S. domination of Iraq before the war, it is hard to see that there was a just intent in pursuing this war. If the intent were to establish a democracy in the heart of the Arab Middle East to promote revolutionary change in Arab regimes, that appears to have been an illusion. Again, the overthrow of the Taliban for the sake of arresting al Qaeda for the series of attacks on the United States can be conceived as a just cause.

Last Resort
It is, of course, hard to determine at what point all other means than war have been exhausted. But there was no threat from Iraq and consequently there remained time for negotiation, or for the United Nation's inspectors to exercise their renewed mandate the search for weapons of mass destruction. Iraq was not involved substantially with the U.S. enemy, al Quaeda. There was more time to return to the United Nations for authority to undertake a U.N. action if the argument could be made that Iraq was a threat to peace. The rush to war seemed to hang upon the findings that Iraq was close to having the capacity to put weapons of mass destruction into operation. That judgment was incorrect. It was unwise to put great confidence in an unknown informant codenamed Curveball. Even more to the point, the United States was engaged in one war in Afghanistan and it desperately needed to finish that war and to crush al Qaeda before undertaking another difficult war. The timing was neither wise nor was it a moment of last resort. The Afghanistan invasion was another matter as the United States did not begin the conflict, but was pursuing enemies who had struck U.S. embassies, a warship, the World Trade Towers, and the Pentagon. Even so the United States demanded the Taliban apprehend al Qaeda before it struck and presumably the Taliban could have avoided the invasion by complying.

Lawful Declaration
Under the U.N. Charter nations renounce the right to war unless sanctioned by the U.N. except for self-defense and then the action must be reported to the U.N. for approval. The Afghanistan invasion had the support of the United Nations and therefore all of the legitimacy it required. The invasion of Iraq is debatable. The first resolution on Iraq gave the United States quite a bit of leeway regarding Iraq, but France and many nations believed that the United States lacked U.N. authorization to invade. Later the U.N. did sanction the coalition occupation forces for a limited period.

Limited Objectives
The ambiguity about the original objectives makes it hard to state whether this criterion has been met or not. The seizure of weapons of mass destruc-

tion would have been a limited objective as would have been breaking the ties between Iraq and al Qaeda, but these were illusory. The creation of a new form of government for Iraq as an influence on the Middle East drifts toward relatively unlimited objectives which are probably impossible to reach. This is part of the debate between realists and neo-conservatives. Limited objectives help keep the use of violence down because limited objectives at least theoretically require proportionately less force to achieve. In both cases, Iraq and Afghanistan, however, the overthrow of the governing powers and the institution of new governments reached toward unlimited objectives. In classical just war theory limited objectives has meant that the restoration of peace was the goal; the U.S. objectives have been much broader than the restoration of a peace. The ambiguity about the original objectives makes it hard to state whether this criterion has been met.

Limited Means

Limited means has meant that civilians were not directly attacked, and that the means used in the war were proportional to the hurt suffered or the wrong being corrected. Modern warfare during World War II and following it has not been careful of civilians; in fact they have been subjected to direct and ruthless attack. In modern warfare most casualties have been civilians. Terrorism is inherently wrong in that it attacks civilians for the creation of fear to serve political purposes. But counterterrorist forces have not refrained from killing civilians either. The United States does limit its means of warfare, and it tries to refrain from killing civilians, but too many mistakes are made and there are too many civilian deaths in both occupied countries to think this criterion has been met. The debate over torture falls into this category as well. This administration has been less careful than previous administrations to discourage torture. The Secretary of Defense has publicly argued for exemption for the Central Intelligence Agency from regulations forbidding torture. The sweeping up of civilians, without charges, has violated limits that have been regarded as lawful in wartime.

As seen above, the six criteria of the just war theory have been seen to be very rigorous in determining what can be regarded as a just war. The last criterion reveals of course the asymmetry of the ongoing war in Iraq where most of the targets of the resistance to the American occupation of Iraq have been civilians. Estimates of civilian casualties in Iraq have ranged from 30,000 to 100,000 in the spring of 2006. While thousands of these deaths are attributable to U.S. firepower, foreign invaders attacking the occupation forces and their allies have contributed more to the deaths and prolonged the war. Iraqi nationals have killed each other in large numbers. These losses and the ongoing war raise the question what is the status of Moslem thinking about justice in this war.

Jihad

The Moslem concept of *jihad* is not parallel to the Western ideas of just war. It is closer to the Christian idea of crusade, and it is often translated in Western sources as "Holy War." *Crusade* refers to the cross and would be totally inappropriate as a term of translation for jihad. Originally in the Koran *jihad* referred to the disciplined struggle against evil and it has several connotations, all of which can be claimed as appropriate interpretations of jihad. But the meaning of concern here is *jihad* as a religiously sponsored war to defend the Islamic homeland. There are also jihads against polytheists, peoples of the book, or deserters of Islam. But the several being mounted now are defensive wars against infidel invaders, and it is hard for Moslems to resist the struggle.

Islam, like Christianity, claims to be a universal faith with many supporting the idea of a world conversion to faith in Allah. Islam does not posit as fundamental a distinction between church and state as Christianity in America has assumed. Islam furthers theocracy and has traditionally hoped it would become universal. Jihad united Moslems against Arab polytheists, then against Jews, then against Persian Zoroastrians, then against Byzantine Christianity, then Coptic Christianity, and finally Roman Catholic Christianity. Christians had to submit and pay the special tax for non-Moslems, become second-class citizens, or die. Polytheists in theory had two options: submission or death. Such a complete union between war and religion swept the middle regions of the earth producing a population second only to Christianity.

Thirteen hundred years of complex history have produced many interpretations of jihad which do not require explanation for the explorations of the consequences of jihad to the modern West.[2] However there are two important distinctions to record: There is the radical Islamist version which recognizes jihad as a program to defeat all non-Islamic regimes and to install a caliph and sharia, religious law, to govern the world. There is also the version—more traditional since the accommodation of Islam to the reality of non-Islamic states—which would restrict jihad to the protection of the Islamic world. Jihad in the interpretation of some pro-western Imams could even be interpreted to include U.S. defense of the independence of Kuwait against Iraq. But the invasion of Afghanistan and Iraq by the United States unites the two major interpretations of defeat of the infidel and defense of Islam together and tends to place the United States in unenviable position of being seen by millions of Moslems as a threat.

Moslems in most countries reject Osama bin Laden's claims to justification for 9/11 and many would have welcomed his capture or his death. Saddam Hussein—seen as a repressor of Shia Islam—was not beloved either. Religious leaders, both Shia or Sunni, could regard him as a secular tyrant, but still the invasion of these countries is seen by millions as a religious offense calling for jihad. Jihad, as opposed to just war, does not entail a requirement of prospects for a successful conclusion. It is a war fought by many for religious reasons and martyrdom or death can be welcomed in the fulfillment of a religious duty.

The British could defeat the Mogul empire in India in the eighteenth century and the Caliphate of Istanbul in the twentieth century. But eventually they retired from India, producing the greatest slaughter in South Asia between Moslems and Hindus in 1948. They left the Arabian Peninsula in the hands of unstable tyrannies and kingdoms after World War II, and then they gave up rule east of Suez. The occupation of Iraq may be too difficult for young American soldiers to hold against jihad. Yet Islamic religious leadership is restrained from protest by America's allies in Egypt, Jordan, Turkey, Saudi Arabia, and Pakistan as all of these governments are also threatened by radical Islam, and these governments respect U.S. power.

America's allies in the Middle East, except for Israel, negotiate between being unable to support America fully or to attack, thoroughly, their threatening radical Islamists who want to drive the United States out of the Middle East. While recognizing the fraudulence of Osama bin Laden's claim to religious leadership, religious opponents of U.S. presence may be inspired by his attacks and defiance of the infidel and its program of globalization.

Disparate elements of Islam joined in jihad, partially funded by the United States, to drive the Soviet Union infidel out of Afghanistan. The Taliban could never complete their unification of the country as the Northern Alliance held on to the Northeast. They could, however, provide a sanctuary for Osama bin Laden's force which at its core was disaffected Arabs. The Arabs were practicing their own form of jihad against their former allies, the United States, for its support of the Saudi family's role and their foreign presence in the Arabian Peninsula. Osama bin Laden's war is consistent with his need to defeat his former ally, America, and to drive its influence out of the Moslem heartland. Objection to American culture, freedoms, and modernism is secondary. It is the imposition of non-Moslem influence on governments and occupation by the U.S. military forces that is primary. Beyond that the mission of Islam is, of course, either to convert the world or to subdue it.

Some modernist interpretations of Islam would reject the above and interpret the fighting verses of the Koran as intended to guide Moslems only when

Islam is attacked or its mission refused. Mahmud Shaltut, for example, makes a case that Islam can be interpreted as basically peaceful and that fighting is only to protect Islam or its mission. He interprets the Prophet's early victories over the polytheists and the Jews as purely defensive wars. The Prophet's letter to the ruler of Byzantium and Abu Bakr's letter to Persia suggesting they convert to Islam or bear the responsibility for the sins of their people in rejecting Islam were rejected by those rulers disdainfully. Such rejection led to the eventual defeat, from a Moslem perspective, of those empires. "'They did not wait for the enemy to attack them in their own country', he writes, 'for only the foolish would wait to fight in their own homes.'" Islam carried this jihad abroad. Shaltut, an important modern interpreter, tries to persuade his readers that Islam's aim is peace, but of course, it is peace on its terms. In many dialogues with Moslems since 9/11, I have heard it argued that the greater jihad is discipline and the struggle with oneself to make one a more pure Moslem. I accept this interpretation, but the lesser jihad of religious war is the jihad that is relevant to the contemporary struggle. It was also relevant to the suppression of Eastern Christianity and North African Christianity.

Radical Islamists reject the moral and spiritual interpretations of jihad and return to the more classical notions of fighting in the service of God. In considering the meaning of jihad for the foes of the United States it is best to think of it in two ways: (1) A defensive war against Western domination of Islam, and (2) an ongoing worldwide revolution for freedom of religion under the rule of Sharia. According to Rudolph Peters jihad can be called for to:

(1) Strengthen monotheism and destroy polytheism;
(2) Protect the mission of Islam;
(3) Repel aggression against Moslems;
(4) Overcome oppression of Moslems outside of Islamic countries;
(5) Revenge a breaking of a treaty.

Modernists stress the defensive functions of jihad and radical Islamists stress both the defensive and expansionist interpretations of jihad. The radical Islamist movements sound somewhat like the liberationists in international relations theory, and somewhat like traditional Christian missionaries who expected the conversion of the world.

James T. Johnson[3] concluded his pre 9/11 study hoping that conflicts between the two worlds could be alleviated as the role of "Holy War" was decreased in Islam as in the West, and as the Western political thought became more aware of the role of religion in international politics. Professor Johnson's optimism was not fulfilled. Various followers of Islam launched holy wars and Western policy makers were very slow to understand the various roles of religion in statecraft. However, his study explained that Moslem holy war had limits. The Prophet and later Moslem thinkers demanded the sparing of women, children, and old men. Johnson finds their mercy to be functional—they did not bear arms, and therefore they should be allowed to live. Even those who bore arms could be spared if they were of value as slaves; if not they could be killed. The rules were not absolute: cities could still be attacked even though non-warriors would be killed. A further limitation was the war was not to be waged by falsehood, the breaking of treaties, or betrayal.

Western thinkers also permitted the enslaving of captured civilians or combatants. The Islam thinking was more developed vis-à-vis Islamic conflict with non-Moslems, and Christianity's protections were for internal conflicts within Christendom. Barbarism in killing civilians had little restraint in the Crusades. The Western prohibition against killing civilians was more absolute than the Islamic rules within their territory but less so than the Islamic restraints in their wars with Islam. However the religious wars faded in the West while the canons of religious war remain normative for Islam according to Johnson's study. For both cultures normative rules are often violated in practice.

The war of the 1980s between Iraq and Iran was for the Shia population of Iran a religious war.[4] As Ruhollah Khomeini had drawn upon the mythology of the origins of Shia to overthrow the Shah, so they enlisted the spirits of their martyred founders against Iraq. The foreign policies of both President Carter and President Reagan were foiled by the Shia holy wars. Martyrdom is essential to Shia which is the faith of the martyred Ali. Ali, according to Shia interpretation, was the rightful heir to Mohammed. The Umayyads usurped his place and then martyred Ali. His grandson Husayn and his followers were defeated and martyred in the battle at Karbala which became the most holy city of Shia Islam. The commitments of Iran to clear the Middle East of American influence are clear. As the war by Shia against Saddam Hussein's rule in Iraq was a holy war, so there are only weak restraining strings keeping the Shia campaign to control Iraq now from moving the shadow civil war into a jihad between Sunnis and Shia. The American army is between the Sunnis and the Shia, and the massive forces of Shia Iran are just across the border. Shia religious leaders and the secular interests of Iran in Iraq are meddling now in Iraq. As I wrote in a 1988 publication,[5] the founding of Shia Islam in martyrdom and war must be taken seriously by anyone who would meddle in the politics of the region. The perspective of Vali Nasr,[6] now a professor at the Naval Postgraduate School, of the relevance of the history of Shia and Sunni struggles to everything that happens in the politics between Shia and Sunni in Iraq and between Sunni and Shia in the international politics of Iraq and Iran would have disinclined a wise U.S. administration from ever trying to remake Iraq. It could be that the belated discovery of the religious war in Iraq would enable the United States to understand that its largely Christian army commanded by a born-again Christian elected with the support of fundamentalist and evangelical Christians cannot impose its will in the middle of the Moslem heartland. The reflection on the just war concepts persuade many that the war should never have been begun. The United States needs to leave Iraq not only because it failed there, but more fundamentally it should never have initiated the war. Once one realizes that the moral tradition regarding war does not find a particular war moral, it behooves the initiating power to act toward ending the war. This does not mean that a nation should engage in a withdrawal from the war precipitously, but it means that it should prudently end the conflict it has begun. To withdraw from Iraq does not mean to end the attempt to bring al Qaeda to justice and to end its depravations. The realization of the religious nature of the wars we are engaged in within Iraq should also provide a major reason for withdrawal of the United States forces.

Notes

1. Arthur Holmes, *War and Christian Ethics: Classic and Contemporary Readings on the Morality of War* (Grand Rapids, MI: Baker Academic, 2005).

2. The most clear study of the background of the definitions between modernist, classical, and fundamentalist interpretations of jihad was Rudolph Peters, *Jihad in Classical and Modern Islam* (Princeton, NJ: Markus Wiener Publishers, 1996). It contains Mahmud Shaltut's treatise "Koran and Fighting," 59–101. Classical interpretations of jihad are clearly expounded in Majice Khadoluri, *War and Peace in the Law of Islam* (Baltimore: John Hopkins Press, 1955).

3. James Turner Johnson, *The Holy War Idea in Western and Islamic Traditions* (University Park: The Pennsylvania State University Press, 1997) hoped at the time of writing for changes in both the West and in Islam.

4. M.J. Akbar, *The Shade of Swords* (New York: Routledge, 2001) brings the discussion of jihad into the Second Gulf War. Rauwen Firestone, *Jihad* (New York: Oxford University Press, 1999) shows the disagreements in the early Moslem community concerning jihad.

5. Ronald H. Stone, *Christian Realism and Peace Making* (Nashville: Abingdon Press, 1988). The book argued for realistic prudence in fighting the campaign against terrorism within the just war rules. It called for both increased protection for embassies and increased security on airplanes. Its focus at the time was on religious aspects of Shia Islam's jihad with the West, and it did not discuss the Sunni struggles of Osama bin Laden against the West, nor did it foresee the deterioration of Saddam Hussein's relationship with the United States which would lead to two wars.

6. Nasr, *Shia Revival*.

CHAPTER THREE

~

Just Peacemaking Theory

Recently a group of ethicists and political scientists have worked together toward a just peacemaking theory. This recent work was preceded fifty years ago by the Federal Council of Churches' Principles for a Just and Durable Peace, and many churches have called for an approach to the issues of war and peace in terms of a just peacemaking emphasis. Glen Stassen, son of the former governor of Minnesota and a professor at Fuller Theological Seminary, provided the charisma which launched the project within the Society of Christian Ethics. The group wanted to go beyond religious pacifism and beyond just war theory to articulate practices which helped avoid wars. In the end they came up with ten practices which they believed could reduce the chances of wars from arising.

The group did not promise world peace. Such hope is reserved for beauty pageant contestants, prayers, and utopian thinkers. The Bible is too realistic to offer such hopes for history. The consultations and publication were completed in 1998 in the post–Cold War window of optimism. Professor Stassen has been deepening the realism of his writing and speaking on the subject. I participated in the project and endorse the concept and program of just peacemaking, but I did not write any of the chapters for the book *Just Peacemaking: Ten Practices for Abolishing War*[1] and I consistently argued we were not being realistic enough about our hopes.[2] No matter how we practice peacemaking a Saddam Hussein may always start a war with Iran or invade Kuwait. An Osama bin Laden may always strike in unsuspected ways of terror. But peacemaking organizations have learned many things and these ten practices are offered as ways beyond either just war or pacifism to approach peace thinking about practice.

The first practice recommended is the *support of nonviolent direct action*. John Cartwright and Susan Thistlewaite wrote about organizing action in the spirit of Ghandhi and King for social change toward peace. The theory and practice of these forms of organization is very developed and the authors discuss boycotts, strikes, marches, civil disobedience, public exposure of false information, accompanying of people threatened by violence, and sanctuary places. These strategies should be attempted before any resort to violence as a last resort can be attempted. In the particular tradition in which I stand a high priority is attached to participation in the political process and on the detailed discussions around divestment from companies profiting from injustice and war. Much of what the authors discussed under boycotts was initiated first by a campaign for divestment which needs to be distinguished from boycotts. Another factor bearing more analysis is the dangers of built up tension encouraged by nonviolent action. Both Ghandi and King were martyred. The 1948 massacres surrounding Indian and Pakistani independence were the worse conflicts between Moslems and Hindus in modern times. The riots in American cities following the 1968 murder of King were the most widespread violent civil disorder in U.S. cities since the Civil War.

Reinforcing the argument for nonviolent direct action is the overwhelming success of nonviolent massive civil disobedience and demonstration in overthrowing the Communist regimes of Eastern Europe and in breaking up the Soviet Empire. The results of nonviolent tactics when used massively are amazing, and our increased use of nonviolent civilian power is one of the good lessons for social action in the twenty-first century.

Glen Stassen wrote the chapter on taking independent initiatives to reduce threat. The emphasis is on nations taking actions to decrease distrust and fear on the part of the other side. Such initiatives helped both the Soviet Union and the United States to back away from war. Independent initiatives can be accompanied by policies of firmness and defense of national interests. Much of the disaster of international relations is based on misperception. Robert Jervis' book *Perception and Misperception in International Politics* is utilized by Stassen in arguing for both reducing conflicts and firmness in national security. Somehow Chairman Khruschev underestimated President Kennedy's firmness when he risked the Cuban missile crisis. Similarly President Bush's ambassador failed the nation when she did not make clear to President Hussein the vital nature of Kuwait's oil to the United States' perceived national interest.

Four members of the group—David Steele, Steven Brion-Meisels, Gary Gunderson, and Edward Long, Jr.—combined their efforts in the chapter on use of cooperative conflict resolution. The process of cooperative conflict resolution (CCR) looks to build partnerships in seeking outcomes that benefit both parties in a conflict. It has application in family, community, political, and international conflicts. The chapter is enriched both by the presentation of the ten points of the CCR method and historical reflection on its use by David Steel in the former Yugoslavia. Its methods can contribute to diplomacy which is a key component in a realist approach to international conflict. For unclear reasons the chapter diverts its approach by using three pages to argue with realism. It portrays realism as a major critic of CCR, but I do not think that the major realist thinkers Reinhold Niebuhr, Hans Morgenthau, John C. Bennett, Arthur Schlessinger, Jr., and Kenneth Thomson attacked CCR. Nor can I concur that realist theory operates with the "'prisoner's dilemma' in game theory." Realism's stress on partnership in managing nuclear weapons with the Soviet Union, the emphasis upon diplomacy, cross-cultural understanding, and history all seem compatible with CCR. Even the theorists claimed in the essay as sources, Jimmy Carter and Martin Luther King, Jr., are not understandable without their respective grounding in the realism of their self-confessed mentor, Reinhold Niebuhr.

Alan Geyer contributed to analyzing the practices of acknowledging responsibility for conflict and seeking repentance and forgiveness. He drew upon his own efforts to help the United States to apologize to Iran for the United States' 1953 intervention in Iran restoring the Shah and other offenses to expedite a reconciliation process for President Carter with Iran to free the hostages. He also built upon Donald Shriver's arguments in *An Ethic for Enemies: Forgiveness in Politics* to show that apology and forgiveness does promote reconciliation and peace. I have argued elsewhere that forgiveness, repentance, and confession are rare in international politics and they normally follow wars (at least in Shriver's examples) rather than prevent wars. Geyer's criticisms of Reinhold Niebuhr were not persuasive to me, but coming in the center of the book following the perspective of the CCR chapter they illustrated the volume's transcendence of the perspectives of realism.

Bruce Russett's chapter on the contribution of advancing democracy, human rights, and religious liberty to peacemaking represents one of the more hopefully liberal chapters in the volume. Written in a time of optimism, he could see expanding international institutions, more free trade, and the numbers of democratic nations increasing all promoting a larger sphere of peace. As a leader in the field of democratic peace research, he concludes the democracies seldom fight among themselves, fight wars that they can win, and dedicate less of their gross domestic product to military expenditures than authoritarian countries. Praising Kant's vision of peace founded upon international institutions, international economic cooperation, and democratic government he argues that it is better to stress the degree of cooperation possible among democracies than to regard every nation as a potential enemy. He may be arguing with a straw opponent here that he labels "extreme realism." It is hard to think of major realist theorists in the United States that would regard American democratic allies as enemies. Realism too seeks cooperation and peace, but it does not engage in the optimism of a Kantian position which Russett affirms. There is deep resistance to the pillars of Russett's argument for religious liberty, human rights, and democracy. The realization of these goals for Iran or Saudi Arabia would require domestic revolutions and replacement of governing elites or crusades from the outside world. Russett warned against the dangers of crusades. He wrote:

> The model of "fight them, beat them, and then make them democratic'" is no model for contemporary action. It probably would not work, and no one is prepared to make the kind of effort that would be required." (104)

But the United States was only one election and one terrorist attack away from adopting the model. Buoyed by victory in the Cold War a new group of neoconservative thinkers and a president dependent upon a right-wing religious coalition would attempt the very policy that Russett thought no one would attempt. The thesis based upon empirical research of a democratic peace would be adopted as a slogan for war in a region beyond the capacity of the United States to dominate. Whereas Russett rightly noted the American policy after World War II was to promote international institutions, human rights, and economic interdependence, the policies of the United States after the fall of the Soviet Union in the George W. Bush administration were to neglect the development of international institutions to attempt to dominate the world militarily, tread heavily upon human rights domestically and internationally, while promoting laissez-faire economics internationally. Religion regarded by Russett benignly was, after the publication of the volume, a much more ambiguous force promoting both good and the ugly. Drifts toward exclusive religious claims whether by Moslems or Christians were translated into military actions, and the liberalization supporting Russett's arguments went into decline both in the United States and the Middle East. The challenge to the Washington consensus in economics particularly in Latin America shows that not only religion, but trends in economics, international organizations, and the foreign policies of democracies are all inherently ambiguous and not necessarily promotive of just peacemaking.

The essay on fostering just, sustainable economic development by David Bronkema, David Lumsdaine, and Rodger A. Payne combines the ecological and humanitarian concerns of development thought that now characterizes development discussions. The group did not share optimism about international organizational macroeconomic projects rather, favoring the nongovernmental organizational approaches that were able to place humane concerns in sustainable development first. They did not argue that more developed economies would be more peaceful countries. Rather they supported the broad meanings of peace that include well-being and healthy relationships as possible fruits from careful, sustainable development strategies. They recognized the need for giving the poor themselves a central role in planning and carrying out development strategies. Human-based development work is good in its own right whether it contributes to international peace or not. On the face of it, the difficulty of arguing that economic development will promote peace rests in the sense that currently developed nations seem to be adept at engaging in war. The coalition involved in occupying Iraq does not consist of economic undeveloped nations. The formerly poor Russia was less belligerent than the more economically solid Soviet Union, and U.S. wealth gives it the capacity to provide other countries with weapons and to undertake risky military adventures itself. The essay advances over too much writing on development which focuses only on economics and overly emphasizes government or international development agencies rather than the nongovernmental programs and the resources of the poor people themselves. The low priority attached to the development of the poor by the current U.S. administration flies against the post–World War II consensus to rebuild Europe and create institutions for economic development of the world. The efforts were better rewarded in Europe than in the Third World. Assaults upon the environment continue in the race for economic development of many economies, and too often the ruling elites of poor nations and developed nations benefit from the status quo and refuse taking significant steps toward development or changing the power realities which hinder real human development.

Historian Paul W. Schroeder urges working with emerging cooperative forces in the international system in his essay. Recognizing the anarchy of the international state system, he still can not wish it away. The contemporary world presented more opportunity to develop institutions of international cooperation than had previous times within the international system. More trade and tighter webs of international institutions can reduce the tendency toward war. Present economic considerations make it less and less valuable for any nation-state to engage in war rationally. Given a perspective of rational choice theory, wars are less likely to appear rational now than they have before, and developing voluntary associations of nations for various purposes will reduce the utility of war even more. So cooperating with the trends toward greater world integration makes sense for peacemakers. Schroeder thinks that within the evolving system cooperation and voluntary associations with standards for enforcing peace have a better chance to preserve peace than heretofore. This was due to the enormous counter-productive cost of war, the rise of the trading state, the increase of the volume of communications, and the gradual ascendancy of democratic governments. While sober minded, the 1998 essay was superseded by his 2004 address to the Society of Christian Ethics in which he deplored the United States imperialism, and called for the defeat of the U.S. policy of domination and war in Iraq. Too many of the trends promoted by the United States after the election of George W. Bush were counter to the productive trends that Schroeder had wanted to cooperate with for the sake of peace. Recent trends in U.S. foreign policy have alternated between the benign neglect of the Clinton administration and the military imperialism of the second Bush administration.

Michael Joseph Smith's essay urges strengthening the United Nations and international efforts for cooperation and human rights. With the cold war over and the Rwandan atrocity staring the world in the face, the case for international humanitarian rescue is made by Smith at the same time it is being discussed by mainline churches. Means to combat genocide overriding national sovereignty needed to be found, and Smith's essay argues the case. He urged in the conclusion a step beyond where nations were likely to go in his advocacy of "a revitalized United Nations equipped with a standing volunteer military force." The tension between sovereignty and the need for international cooperation and action shifts, and the United States is currently pushing it in the direction of U.S. sovereignty and the potential for full military domination. The international system will eventually counteract that push. It is unlikely, though, that the U.N. will be granted military standing beyond its present voluntary subscription of forces with the U.N. continuing to lack intelligence and command and control capabilities. This is not to suggest that the need for more U.N. peacekeeping and peacemaking actions may not increase. As with other proposals to strengthen the U.N., its members withhold the resources even while in some cases wishing the U.N. could accomplish more. The nations refuse to give the U.N. the sovereignty and the revenue that it would need to accomplish its missions of peacemaking.

Barbara Green and Glen Stassen join in explicating the ninth practice to reduce offensive weapons and weapons trade. The authors explain the obstacles confronting reductions in arms trade as well as possibilities for reducing the trade. Unfortunately the U.S. over-response to 9/11 resulted in many restraints in U.S. shipments of arms being dropped as regimes violating human rights were opened to arms subsidies and sales if they were regarded as allies in the "War on Terrorism." So regardless of Pakistan's abridgement of human rights and sharing of nuclear technology with Iran, Libya, and Korea, arms were supplied to this country harboring Osama bin Laden and the Taliban. The United States remains the largest exporter of weapons and the sales grew particularly in the Near East and India. An updating of the excellent essay, completed in 1997, would show decline in most of the favorable trends recorded at that point. The appeal for leadership in reducing the provision of weapons, often with subsidies for purchase and training is appropriate and would contribute to peacemaking The challenge of the military-industrial complex to rationality in foreign policy remains as significant as it did at the time of President Eisenhower's Cold War speech in 1961. Mostly at the tax payers' expense the United States armed both the new nuclear weapon states of Pakistan-India and the old opponent of Israel-Egypt. U.S. troops suffer at the firepower of U.S. weapons provided in Iraq and Somalia, and dictators suppress opposition throughout the world with U.S.-provided arms. In remaining the largest supplier of weapons to poor developing nations the United States appears to be assuming the role of an imperial power arming whom it will with tanks, helicopters, missiles, small arms, ships, and artillery.

While understanding that reducing the arms trade would be a peacemaking practice at this point in history, it seems to be more of a critical principle than a practice. The reading of the chapter in 2008 promotes pessimism bordering on cynicism about the arms trade, and the statistics from Congress in the "Conventional Arms Transfers to Developing Nations, 1997–2004" released on August of 2005 deepens the pessimism. Real progress in reductions of arms trade waits upon political progress and the lowering of tensions even though reductions in arms buildups would contribute to relaxing tensions. Meanwhile reductions of weapons of mass destruction are given as reasons for war in Iraq and produce major conflicts with North Korea and Iran.

North Korea has joined the nuclear weapons club most recently along with Pakistan and India. The United States tries valiantly to deter Iran away from nuclear weapons. While this diplomatic game was unfolding, Hans Blix's committee reported to U.N. Secretary-General Kofi Anan in June of 2006. The committee called for the United States to lead in reducing nuclear weapons.

The committee's findings supported the arguments about nuclear weapons in the just peacemaking approach. U.S. actions in not ratifying the test ban treaty in 2002 and withdrawing from the Anti-Ballistic Missile Treaty of 1972 were accompanied by cynicism about international agreements to limit arms by the superpower. As international agreements were abandoned, unilateral proliferation spread. Blix recommended outlawing nuclear weapons, and he urged movement away from high-alert status for the weapons and called for pledges of no first use. The committee reported on 27,000 nuclear weapons with 12,000 of them deployed around the world.[4]

In the final essay Duane K. Friesen argues for the importance of encouraging grassroots peacemaking groups and voluntary associations. All peacemaking work requires organization. Part of the need of just peacemaking is to have it taught, but beyond that it needs mass support. The power of nonviolent action has been demonstrated, most recently in the collapse of the Soviet Empire, and similar efforts of passion and organization will be required to demilitarize the American empire. Peace lobbies, organizations, and voices can dissuade the United States from some of its more risky policies. The country cannot afford $500 billion military budgets, and the 200 million spent per day in Iraq. The Pentagon supports between 6,000 and 7,000 sales people to push arms sales and the largest companies in the United States make much of their easiest profits from war material. Organizations to reduce the Leviathan to reasonable proportions require the churches and nongovernmental organizations of all types. Often the grassroots groups still need to be organized while the existing networks need volunteers and resources. Once a vision of peacemaking is grasped the next requirement is organization.

Stassen has argued persuasively in both academic and church journals that just peacemaking practices are an alternative to many wars.[5] The alternative to the occupation of Iraq was to allow the international inspections under Hans Blix to continue, to continue to patrol the skies of Iraq, and to encourage slow processes of Iraq resistance to attempt to bring Saddam Hussein down within their own time and capacity to act while protecting Kurds and southern independence movements as they developed autonomy. This of course presupposes that the elder Bush had already gone to war with Iraq once and that President Clinton had continued the containment of Iraq. The roots of the occupation are in the first war with Iraq. The facts point, I believe, to the need of better diplomacy[6] as I am persuaded that Hussein was allowed to misperceive the vital interest the United States had in not permitting Iraq to dominate Kuwait and to affect the balance of power in the Gulf. Structurally the U.S. economy is organized to require access to Gulf oil. It should not be so. Also the international cooperation, law, and institutions required by just peacemaking theory are not affirmed by the current leaders of the United States. So to return to the threefold analysis of why war happens: failures in leadership, national structures, and international anarchy all make war and the attempted military dominance of the Gulf by the United States likely. Good will and the insights of just peacemaking theory could have gone a long way toward preventing the Second Gulf War, but the first war was largely a failure of diplomatic communication. The will for peace on the part of United States was not strong enough in U.S. leadership which wanted war before 9/11, so the results of the election of 2000 almost made the war in Iraq inevitable and foolish. According to al Qaeda their war with the United States was due to the U.S. operations in the Gulf region and in particular in Saudi Arabia during the First Gulf War as well as the religious conflict over the use of the Temple Mount in Jerusalem and Sharon's incursion there. While statements from al Qaeda are as subject to distortion or deliberate distortions as other statements about motivation, substantial clues to al Qaeda's behavior are present in their role in internal Saudi Arabian politics and economy. In any case it is important to remember it was Saudis not Iraqis who attacked the United States and that al Qaeda had its refuge in Afghanistan and Pakistan and not in Iraq.

The Taliban who ran Afghanistan according to their interpretation of Islamic law lost their battle to defend Osama bin Laden in Afghanistan. But this group named for a theological student's movement is now cooperating in Pakistan with the Inter-Services Intelligence to send students from Pakistani theological schools back into Afghanistan in jihad against the NATO forces. The religious parties have joined with secret services in Pakistan to support each other's interests including war in Kashmir and Afghanistan. The Father of one of the jihadists saw his son who had disappeared from his madrasa:

> "He had a shawl over his head and was preparing for a suicide bombing," Mr Gaul said. He said, "I am fighting for God and I am ready for this."[7]

Mahmoud M. Ayoub's conclusions to his study *Islam Faith and History* are helpful in understanding jihad here:

> Islam is not a religion of violence, but a religion of power. This includes military, political, economic, and social power....jihad may at times require armed struggle, but armed struggle must always be a means, and not an end in itself.[8]

Once the case is made for armed struggle the religion of Islam can be used to recruit either armed forces or terrorists. From America the ideology of neoconservative will to dominance similarly can be used to recruit armed forces or to provide for mercenaries recruited by private companies to help insure that dominance using their own methods and violence. Both the Taliban and the American neoconservative thinkers who planned to invade Iraq before 9/11 occurred probably are beyond the reaches of just peacemaking theory.

Notes

1. Glen Stassen, ed., *Just Peacemaking: Ten Practices for Abolishing War* (Cleveland: Pilgrim Press, 1998).

2. I published an essay which was more critical of just peacemaking than this chapter which is largely exposition as "Realist Criticism of Just Peacemaking Theory," *The Journal of the Society of Christian Ethics* (Sping/Summer 2003) 255–64.

3. Stassen, *Just Peacemaking*, 104.

4. Warren Hoge, "U.N. Report Calls for U.S. Leadership on Nuclear Disarmament," *Pittsburgh Post Gazette* June 2, 2006. A4.

5. Glen Stassen. "'Yes' to Just Peacemaking, Not Just 'No' to War," *Church & Society* November/December, 2005, 64–81.

6. Among sources on the need for better diplomacy, I have found John D. Stumpel, "Recasting Diplomacy" to be particularly helpful. Unpublished Manuscript. Oct. 1994. See also: Morgenthau, *Politics Among Nations*, 519–550.

7. "At Border Signs of Pakistan Role in Taliban Surge," *The New York Times* (Jan.31, 2007) 12.

8. Mahmoud M. Ayoub, *Islam faith and History* (Oxford: One World Publications, 2004) 228.

~

CHAPTER FOUR

Religion, Morality,
and International Politics

The preceding discussion has presented ideas about the relationship of religious ethics to international politics focusing on the case of American policy vis-à-vis Iraq since 9/11. Deeper inquiry takes this discussion into the meaning of religion itself as well as its relationship to morals and international politics.

A personal word helps to identify the perspective from which this chapter is written. In 1968, I was teaching two courses at Columbia University and one on moral issues in international politics at Union Theological Seminary. At Union we were secure in faith and assumed its applicability to international affairs. At Columbia one of my courses in contemporary civilization concluded the required curriculum studying books by Sigmund Freud, Friedrich Nietzsche, and Karl Marx that were critical of Western forms of faith and civilization. The course I taught in world religions had the relativity of religions built into it because each religion was presented in the context of many of the different perspectives of religious thinking and practice. These three influences of Western enlightenment criticizing religion, the relevance and relativity of all religions, and the security of Christian faith inform this analysis. The turmoil at Columbia and Union in the student revolutions conditioned the turmoil of a young assistant professor's life in New York City. The resultant move was to take the turmoil and the various presuppositions to Pittsburgh Theological Seminary and the University of Pittsburgh for a lifetime of teaching and research in politics, morals, and religion from 1969 to 2005.

Of the three critics from Central Europe, I studied Karl Marx most deeply though I read widely in the other two, and I owe Freud more than Nietzsche who was the first philosopher I studied as an undergraduate. World religions disagreed on as much as they agreed upon. The debts of the perspectives to their respective histories, geographies, and experience of both founders and interpreters force one to take a relative perspective on each major system simply to study or teach them. The different systems of religious ideas, rituals, and ethics revealed that all could be explained as complex human constructs to meet human experience and needs. The antiquity of religious expression in burial and art practices joined with the near universality of religion to support its own claims of significance. Genealogical, psychological, or economical critiques of religion did not prove religion to be all illusion, but rather almost universally human. The relativity of the perspectives of Nietzsche, Freud, and Marx were as obvious as the relativity of religion. All were human constructions which had evolved through time to their present state of practice or criticism.

Both religion and the spiritualities arising from it meet more or less human needs for awe, reverence, community, ritual, ethics, and encountering meaning in the stages of life especially death. They usually express powers of the human brain to transcend immediate experience, while promoting it to ask questions of meaning, transformation, or salvation, and answers to human dependence upon the universe or its spirit or spirits. Religions function in this constructed human reality because of their congruence with the brain and its place in the universe. Whether we reflect upon the religious meaning of Stone Age cave paintings or the pyramids of Egypt, or a prayer breakfast in the U.S. capital, we know that all capture enough of a resonance with human need to have the effects reflect in their work and artifacts.

Major religions have evolved through time as every student of religion knows. The uninformed religious masses may not know that the religious expression of Moses is quite different from that of Augustine but every scholar or even every careful reader of the two grasps the radical differences as well as some similarities. Of course, Moses is presented differently even within different layers of the Bible. Augustine is interpreted radically differently by Protestants and Roman Catholics. Religious traditions continue to change through time even though contemporaries may not know the extent to which their interpreters modify the tradition as they change it from one generation to another. Current debates within Protestantism and Catholicism concerning the ordination of homosexuals reflect the capacity of religious traditions to change and to resist change. Similar issues regarding change were at stake in the debates over ordaining women within the last century.

Religious innovations often seem to stem from the experience of one person like Abraham, Moses, Jesus, Paul, Luther, Mohammed, and Buddha, but these expressions can only come alive in believers through human interpretation. The recording of the interpretations in scripture leads to further interpretation. Experiences are mixed with ritual and ancient mythologies to weave current psychological, political, and economic needs into complex systems of ideas. Historical moments interpreted in religious terms become myths as the meaning of history is explicated. Particular symbols found to contain meaning are woven together in reformulated myths and sometimes passed from one culture to another where fresh meaning is attached. The Abrahamic faiths illustrate the process, the Christian New Testament uses Hebrew scriptures in ways foreign to Judaism, and Islam utilizes both Hebrew and Christian scripture in ways strange to both traditions.

When Christianity, Buddhism, Confucianism, and animism are all considered religions, religion itself is very hard to define. The group of young religion instructors at Columbia tried a variety of definitions for consideration in 1968 for teaching several sections of the world religions course. One attempted to define religion as: "Phenomena you would not laugh about." Paul Tillich's definition of religion as that which concerned one ultimately seemed to be as close to an agreed-upon definition as the instructors could come to that year.

"Ultimate concern" captures the seriousness of religion and points toward the reality of the religious person and also toward a reality of the ultimate. Not all religious groups could accept the definition, but it is suggestive for Christianity, Judaism, and Islam with their emphasis upon creation, dependence, salvation, and judgment. Perhaps ultimate concern sounds too individualistic for the history of religion and more like the expression of disconnected late-twentieth-century spirituality. If so, Tillich's own understanding of religion as the depth of the culture is a corrective. Perhaps to capture the social reality of religion it should be defined as the organized responses of humans to their ultimate concerns.

There is a clue even in the word *organized*. The human needs for security, food, and meaning gradually diverged in urban civilization when there were agricultural resources to support separate religions and military organizations. The rulers or emperors could come from either group and their relations took many different dialectical forms. Those who supplied the surpluses off of which the military and religious leaders lived seldom achieved dominance until modern times resulted in the middle class controlling much of the means of production. All sorts of arrangements evolved as the needs to organize protection and meaning systems related through the centuries. The attempt to privatize religion characteristic of the secular enlightenment of Western Europe is only one way to handle the relationship and the new secular order of the

American republic was a rather extreme example of that attempt. The evangelical awakening of the late twentieth and early twenty-first century in the United States threatens to undo that predominantly secular interpretation of the state. Likewise the movement in the Middle Eastern countries to overthrow secular governments who control Islam and replace them with Islamic law or Sharia has received new energy in the late last century. But to date the secular governments hold out except in the cases of Iran and Sudan. Religious enthusiasts of a particularly militant type threaten from both the United States and the Middle East to involve the two civilizations in armed struggle.

As far as we can tell, that which we designate religion was not distinguished from other aspects of life in primitive societies. Life was less complex and less specialized and religion permeated most aspects of life: cooking, hunting, agriculture, morals, governance, and war. The word itself is a Western word of Latin derivation and its use to distinguish certain aspects of life from the more mundane or secular operations occurred in the West which distinguished more sharply between church and state than did the Eastern world.

The modern experience of the West in setting certain practices aside as religion while allocating most of life as secular seems strange to more traditional minds and it is resisted by many religiously sensitive people in the West as well. It is a practically alien concept to the masses of Moslems affected by U.S. policies in the Middle East. One needs to add that its radical forms are separations unknown to the religious expressions of the Bible.

The separation of religion and morality is an extreme development for they originated in the human mind and practice together. Most ancient moral codes were attributed to the deities of the culture. It is often remarked the Confucian ethics are an exception as they are so secular and political, but even the Confucian ethical way is under the mandate of the Heaven. Also most Confucians also practice another religion as well. In the West since the Enlightenment and even in some Greek predecessors morality seems to be based on reason or on nature and it is only minimally religious. But neither the ethics of Kant nor Hegel stray very far from their Western religious roots. Marx, Freud, and Nietzsche made more substantial breaks, but they undercut moral wisdom rather than contributed to it. However ethics as the critical thought about what is right, good, and just has also reformulated religion. From Amos to the present, sharp ethical critique has criticized religion and tried to make it more humane and more justice serving. In the United States organized religion and its satellites seem to be the major forces undergirding public morality with all of its strengths and weaknesses. Many religious bodies in the United States tend to express their social policies in public ethical debate. That is helpful for political discussion because no one is privileged in the public ethical debate. However, other religious groups express their ethical convictions in direct religiously confessional language. They have such a right. As inconvenient it is and even absurd as it is people have the right to claim direct revelation by God for their political opinions by dint of Biblical interpretation or wisdom. Those who disagree can try and persuade them or resort to voting against them. Usually in political debate whether couched in Biblical or rational argument organized group interest is barely hidden in the arguments.

Because political argument is so often about self or group interest over who gets what and when and how, its moral purity is compromised. Very little in politics is pure or rational. So sensitive religious persons cannot help but act politically, but the very religious conviction which impels them to act urges them to act circumspectly. It is best usually to put the prestige of one's religious beliefs only behind political acts of ultimate importance and there are not many of those. It is only presumption to think that the spirit that created the universe is vitally concerned about the placement of a highway or a sewer line. Human safety and ecology may be of concern to the interpreters of the Holy Spirit, but the placement of public works has too many financial implications to be a simple matter of ultimate concern.

So many matters of political concern involve the enrichment of some and the impoverishment of others that generally it is wise to resolve these issues on grounds of political or moral debate without claiming the deity has chosen sides or that an interpretation of scripture supporting one's position is absolute. It is wiser and easier to reach agreements of compromise if the argument is over the just or the greatest good, or the least evil, than it is over ones sacred scriptures. In a republic, of course, the issues are resolved by voting rather than by argument though arguments have influence. At the level of voting whether in the House of Representatives or the local polling both the rule of conscience, whether influenced by reason, religion, or intuition, is only one factor of several and not the strongest factor for most who vote. Congressman John P. Murtha put it:

> You need to get things done so you give them the votes to get the things done. There is no question that some projects come out of it for our members and that is not a bad thing. . . . deal making is what Congress is all about.[1]

Archbishop Donald Wuerl of Washington, D.C., expressed the relationship of faith and politics as:

> The two spheres, church and state while distinct are always interrelated. Politics, law, faith are mingled because believers are also citizens. Church and state are home for the same people.

His words were at a mass celebrating the beginning of a Supreme Court term where for the first time the majority of five judges were Roman Catholics. He also said:

> What we do and how we act, our morals and ethics follow on what we believe....The religious convictions of a people sustain their moral decisions.[2]

The close association of faith and politics is more characteristic of Roman Catholic consensus and of the relatively religious United States than it is of some other systems and most European countries. Utilitarian philosophers and pragmatists like Jeremy Bentham and John Dewey can write creative studies in social ethics and policy while remaining aloof from religious issues. Paul Tillich noted how socialists in European politics were often alienated from church and/or religious perspectives. Enlightenment philosophy and its successive expressions has relied heavily on reason and submerged references to religious faith. He thought there needed to be reforms in both religious and social thought to reconcile socialism and religious life. He hoped, in the 1930s before being dismissed from his role as Dean of Faculty of the University of Frankfurt, for such a reformation to oppose the parareligious movements of Nazism and Communism. Post-war politics and political science paid little attention to church policies or religion until the civil rights movement was organized by Black clergy. John Kennedy's religion and Jimmy Carter's were widely discussed, but only with the assertiveness of the evangelical religious right in the 1970s did it become a popular field of research.

Mainstream denominations, ecumenical Christianity, and leading religious social philosophers like Reinhold Niebuhr had tried to move the country through political analysis, religious values, and social ethics and they advocated transcendence for the most part from direct political involvement by the churches.

The right-wing evangelicals inherited deep distrust of the liberal directions of the country, particularly regarding their understandings of the family values, abortion, sexuality, and so on. When combined with a Republican southern strategy to run against negative perceptions of the Black population and neoconservative fiscal policy of reducing taxes by expanding the national debt this distrust of liberalism became a potent force. Skill in national and local organization produced new voting majorities upon which Republican victories against Jimmy Carter and Democrat candidates were built. The same strategy moved some of the Democrat working class base toward the Republican Party. Democrat Presidential candidates identified as liberals were defeated in the polls or by the courts by this combination. Bill Clinton could prevail, even while religious right-wing organizations deepened their support for the Republican Party, as neither the elder Bush nor Senator Dole presented starkly more religious portraits nor fit the religious right's needs. Clinton's appeal to self-interest, "It's the economy stupid," trumped for a season the values agenda of the religious right's political ambition. The pendulum swung back against the liberals Al Gore and John Kerry with born-again George W. Bush receiving strong religious-right support.

All of this religious political history had its consequences for U.S. foreign policy, and writers like Secretary of State Madeleine Albright[3] and Council on Foreign Relations leader Walter Russell Mead[4] grappled with the issue in important publications. This new emphasis has pushed the issues into public discussions. The subject itself is at least as ancient as the writings of Amos and Isaiah, and it has always received some attention. It was particularly prominent in the writings of Secretary of State John Foster Dulles. Reinhold Niebuhr devoted much of his analysis to the subject of religious ethics and foreign relations and taught a course on the subject. Now the easy dismissal of the relevance of faith to politics or foreign policy is no longer intellectually respectable.

The other force moving religion into consideration is the militant Moslem attempt to displace more secular rulers in the Middle East, and to govern societies by Sharia, Islamic Law. The combination of religious and liberation movements to drive Russians out of Afghanistan has evolved into threats to drive the United States out of the Middle East. Obviously politics, economics, and personal ambitions are all involved in the current struggles. However, on both of the militant Moslem jihads against the United States—the American identification with Israel and the war against the Baathists in Iraq—religious issues are involved. Even American allies like Saudi Arabia pay more attention to religious loyalties in supporting Sunni against Shia than they do to the American political interests.

Religious Idealization

Religion, like romance, lives in part by a process of idealization. The process of idealization focuses love on a person, text, ritual, or community which is idealized. The idealization of objects of love can and often does lead to the profanization of other objects. When religion is mixed with nationalism or other forms of communalism it can lead to demonizing other communities or nations. The Nazi love for the myth of the pure Ayrian led to the myth of the perfidious Jew. Judaism did not fit within the purview of the mythical Aryan German nation. In the contemporary situation Shia Islam mixed with Iranian nationalism can lead Iranian leaders to demonize both the United States and Israel even though realistically many of the Iranian leaders know better. American fundamentalism can divide the world into nations of the axis of evil and democracy even though the relativities of all nation-states are readily apparent. Similarly interpretations of the Bible which disagree with each other can be seen as absolute even when the differences among interpretations are clear to most. Idealization of objects of love is psychologically almost inevitable, but it must be joined by realism which recognizes ambiguities in that which is loved. Romanticism in personal relations and international relations must be qualified by realism for mature relations. Mature religion recognizes there are many religions, with respective strengths and weaknesses. The choosing of one religion like the choosing of one love relationship for a mate, does not require the demonizing of others.

The systematic study of religions like genuine interreligious dialogue fosters the process of seeing religions as relative to their culture and history. This is good. All religions are human constructs reflecting particular histories, experiences, and places. Claims of absolutism in morals and religion reflect over idealization[5] of norms and religious practices. There is no religious need to claim absolute authority for one interpretation of the divine.

Because Hans Kung was correct in his claim that there is no international peace without religious peace, the study of religions is central to the search for peace. It is my experience that one can live in secure faith and peace while knowing that no one interpretation of the truth of the spirit of the universe is final. The dawning upon humanity that religion itself is relative and relational to community, place, and time will assist in the human realization that certain economics and politics are also relative. Many forms of religious-economic-culture-political societies will arise, evolve, and change and the differences among them are not worth wars.

Alan Geyer's Typology

Several decades ago Alan Geyer published an empirically based investigation of the relationship of American religion to American politics, especially international politics.[6] The book has not received the attention it deserved and an exploration of some of its findings helps clarify the issues. He makes use of an examination of American diplomatic history as well as empirical studies of how American political figures have used or reflected religion and how religious emphases and themes as well as actors have influenced American foreign policy. Not surprisingly he finds the traces of Puritan influence to be quite strong in the American character especially in the work ethic, world transforming, and socially realistic perspectives of those ancestors. He jokingly refers to this aspect as the Geyer-Freudian father complex explanation of foreign policy. Interestingly his doctoral research was undertaken at Boston University graduate school where the suspicion about the influence of Puritan fathers might be anticipated. I would not want to take anything away from the perspective he sheds on the Puritan fathers, but I would be inclined to emphasize a little more than he, perhaps, the Enlightenment origins of American politics. John Locke, for example, represents both. And some would emphasize the Presbyterian contribution through John Witherspoon and the James Madison authorship of the Constitution, but that discussion aside, his book is interesting and insightful, and he provides a typology of the relationship of religion to international politics in the American context. He uses the typology or intellectual construction of types of relationships to reveal those patterns which the mass of historical data obscures. Students of social ethics recognize immediately the influence of Max Weber and Ernst Troeltsch in such a construction, and also the work of H. Richard Niebuhr, one of whose typologies was examined in the first chapter. In "an inventory of the relationship of religious influence in world politics" he lists sixty ways that religion influences foreign policy and he also shows pretty consistently throughout the book how terribly complicated the implementation of foreign policy in the United States is. Some of the influences vary from "Source of supranational loyalties," "Action antagonistic to official policy goals," "Source of internal tension for policy-makers," "Component of national ideology," to "Sustainer of military morale." His typology has six types of relationships:

1. Religion as a source of loyalty
2. Religion as a sanction for political loyalty
3. Religion as a sanction for political conflict
4. Religion as a source of political conflict
5. Religion as a sanctuary from political conflict
6. Religion as a reconciler of political conflict

His construction presupposes the reality of conflict in politics and diplomacy, and he affirms the reality of using imagination to resolve conflicts and the possibility of institutionalizing conflict and reducing its destructiveness.

The first role of religion in world politics is in enlisting people's loyalty to a center of loyalties or God. Following that the religious community itself requires loyalty; both of these loyalties can support national policy or lead religious people to dissent from it. The leaders of religious groups do not usually make foreign policy, but as elite participants they may influence foreign policy, and there may be a considerable gap between the judgments of the elite leaders and the population of the group itself.

Second, most religions interpret religious sanctions that enforce loyalty to the government. American people tend to be religious and orthodox in their religious beliefs and these beliefs usually reinforce commitments to the society and the state. Nationalism, which in many ways is an enemy to religion, in the United States tends to reinforce and get reinforced by the popular religions of the country. American democracy developed into a kind of religion complete with suspicion of the state, but also religious commitments to it. Woodrow Wilson and John Foster Dulles were both used by Geyer as examples which merged nationalism with an almost Messianic role for the United States in world politics and internationalism.

Third, religion is often a sanction of conflict. Usually the clergy of the country support the United States' participation in wars. God is preached as on the American side. Often the opponents are portrayed as atheists or nonreligious. The scriptures of both the Old and New Testaments are used to glorify American participation in war, historically as much as any other traditions. The firepower of the American arsenal including the nuclear weapons makes these justifications seem overdrawn to much of the world.

Fourth, religion is sometimes the source of conflicts. It may conflict with the state or it may lead a state or a party within the state into conflict for religious reasons of difference in teaching, practice, or ethnic hatred expressed in religious terms. The student of religion and politics has to recognize that religion is not always positive. It has its complicated origins in the nature of humanity which is very flawed and prone to be the most violent of the creatures on earth. The faith of the Old Testament in the hands of European pioneers in America was used to treat the Native Americans as Philistines who should be destroyed to allow the chosen ones to have the land. Christianity has harbored anti-Judaism, and only now is it being rooted out of Christian literature, preaching, and teaching. The hostility of Catholics and Protestants has not only been economic and political, but really deeply religious, and tolerance was learned only with the Enlightenment for modern Europeans.

Fifth, religion has functioned as a sanctuary or escape from world politics. Christianity transcends world politics, though its central symbol of the cross is deeply involved in religious-political conflict. It can be an escape. It ought to be a real refuge where one can gather strength, learn forgiveness, and renew oneself spiritually away from the fray. Religion may encourage pacifism, privatism, or even a rejection of politics. Religious explanations may obscure the pursuit of political philosophy and science which the most powerful country in the world needs.

Finally, religion can become a help in reconciling conflict. The religious peace movements have value, and international understanding can be promoted because of the international character of the church and its channels of communication. Religious leaders can speak against hate, and for tolerance and justice. Acts of church mercy and support serve the work of reconciliation. Christians and others are called personally to reconcile the clashes of world politics within themselves and their own consciences to engage in the calling to be peacemakers. Church witness for international aid, against overarmament, against racism, and for reconciliation are all part of the opinion base in the population out of which foreign policy in its complex patterns is drawn. In a country as religious as the current United States it is very difficult for foreign policy to be wiser or better than that of its religions. At a time when many are engaged in religious wars and there are those voices in the United States which support war in the name of the deity, the reconciling function is found to be sorely needed.

The strength of Geyer's typology is in its comprehensiveness. With it in mind one has less reason to be surprised by the various forms religion is expressed in world politics. Yet, the Baker Commission report on Iraq as late as 2006 showed little depth in understanding of the religious issues at stake in the war. It did show the unpreparedness of the United States by reporting only 10 out of 1000 diplomatic personnel in the U.S. mission in Iraq could speak Arabic.

In my previous writing on foreign policy related to terrorism, I have emphasized the need for interreligious dialogue with our allies and our enemies. During the Cold War I had spent many trips behind the Iron Curtain dialoguing with Marxists. Sermons on peacemaking were welcomed in Communist countries and lectures dealing with foreign relations and church peacemaking were appreciated in Charles University in Prague and in the Humboldt University in East Berlin. While those engendered some hostile reactions in the United States, a dialogue trip to speak with allies and perceived enemies in the Middle East provoked much stronger hostile and misunderstandings than any trip to speak with Communists during the heat of the Cold War. The following chapter summarizing some of the experiences of a fact-finding tip, including dialogue, to the Middle East shows the difficulties of such openness while still reflecting the lasting conviction that without religious dialogue among the religions including some of the extremist expressions of religion and politics there will be neither peace nor understanding.

Notes

1. David D. Kirkpatrick, "Trading Votes for Pork Across the House Aisle," *The New York Times* (October 2, 2006), 1.

2. Peter Bancrjee, "Archbishop Calls for Court Blessing Steers Clear of Issues," *The New York Times* (October 2, 2006), 12.

3. Madeleine Albright, *The Mighty and the Almighty* (New York: Harper Collins Publishers, 2006).

4. Walter Russell Mead "Religion and U.S. Foreign Policy," *Foreign Affairs* (Sept./Oct. 2006), 24–14.

5. James W. Jones, *Terror and Transformation: The Ambiguity of Religion in Psychiatric Perspective* (New York: Taylor and Francis, Inc., 2002).

6. Alan Geyer, *Piety and Politics: American Protestantism in the World Arena* (Richmond: John Knox Press, 1963).

CHAPTER FIVE

On Speaking to
Hezbollah and a Jewish Settler

A challenge to speak to those called terrorists was laid down at the Stony Point, New York, Peacemaking Conference in the fall of 2004: "Professor Stone since you have written on terrorism, why not go and talk with the terrorists?" Actually events were moving toward that encounter. The Advisory Council on Social Witness of the Presbyterian Church U.S.A. was planning to undertake a fact-finding mission to inform itself about the Middle East so that it could fulfill its task of advising the General Assembly of the Church about social policy. I had chaired the task force on terrorism whose work had been approved by the General Assembly. The report, of course, condemned terrorism for attacking civilians and laid down strategies for combating it in two categories of suppressive and transformative strategies. Terrorism as the attack on noncombatant civilians for political ends was immoral and had to be overcome.

The coordinator of the Social Witness Policy Committee, Peter Sulyok, forewarned a group of theologians of the complications of the trip. After a confrontational discussion with Chicago rabbis over the proposal to divest Presbyterian stockholdings from some companies supporting violence and oppression in Palestine/Israel he led the Theological Educators for Presbyterian Social Witness in a debriefing. One of his questions was: "In a few weeks, Professor Stone will be talking across a table with Chairman Yassir Arafat. What do you advise him to say?" In the Chicago dialogue with the rabbis I had made clear the Presbyterian Church U.S.A.'s opposition to Israel's occupation of Gaza and Palestine and our longstanding commitment to defend

Israel. Furthermore I defended divestment from selected corporations as a viable means of social change and in this case a movement for Israel's own good. On arrival in Lebanon meetings were held with the Near East School of Theology and the National Evangelical Synod of Syria and Lebanon, Executive Committee and the Administrative Council Members. With the encouragement of the Synod and the Middle East Council of Churches the group traveled to Southern Lebanon, worshiped on Sunday with the Presbyterian Church, Ebel Al-Saki, sang the hymn "Amazing Grace" for the church, enjoyed a reception, and continued conversations with Hezbollah representatives who had joined them before the church service.

The Advisory group noticed as they came into South Lebanon that they passed through a Lebanese Army check point and through a Hezbollah check point. Their bus was provided with a Hezbollah car escort throughout the trip to South Lebanon, a courtesy extended in several countries by other governments. The group was aware that the divestment decisions of their General Assembly provided a new context for discussions in the Arab world. They did not realize how well-informed Arab leaders would be about the General Assembly's action.

The government of Lebanon was falling, the Prime Minister resigned the next day, Israeli forces were bombing in Gaza, and the visit was bracketed by suicide bombings in Israel by Palestinians. The Israeli Knesset was proceeding with debates over disengagement in Gaza, and the United States was successfully leading a coalition to pass a United Nation's resolution to pressure Syria to withdraw from Lebanon. The war in Iraq was continuing amid the turmoil of occupation of that country. Our visit was a very small event in the context of ecclesiastical and secular politics in the region. The group had read the *Church and Society* journals of the last two issues and was well informed of General Assembly policy against terrorism, against the Israeli occupation, for human rights, for secure borders for Israel, and for peace. Some understood that the divestment issue was causing a lot of concern in the Louisville headquarters of the church.

At Khiam Detention Center, a former French barracks, then an Israeli prison and now a museum, the group met Sheik Nabil Quaq. He expressed warm greetings to the church group and criticized very forcefully U.S. policy in Iraq and with Israel.

The comments which follow both from the Sheik and from myself are from my notes reconstructed by memory, and they suffer from incompleteness. The Sheik said:

Blessings upon you from our Holy Fathers Abraham, Moses, Jesus, Mohammed. I greet you with the most compassionate, warm greetings. Our land is blessed by your visit and in the name of Jesus Christ who walked in our land we greet you all.

We have suffered grievously from aggression by Israel which was given a green light and still is given a green light by the United States.

We have waited for a word of justice from the United States, but we have heard only silence. The United States covered over the massacre at the camps. It condemned us and judged us. The United States has been negative about Lebanon. It has stirred up sectarian conflict and you are aware of this.

Today, the United States pressures us and our neighbor Syria to stand alongside Israel and its power. In Lebanon we have known freedom and we have known democracy. We have sympathy for the American voters who have to choose between two candidates who both will support Israel to win the support of the American people.

Our argument is not with the American people, but with the political administration which in its arrogance is imposing through force its ideology upon the world. The U.S. policy is one of supporting Sharon's policies of occupation and assassination which are the worse form of terrorism in the world. The United States permits it. We have waited for a word of justice from the United States, but we have heard only silence. The United States is suspicious of everyone. Muslims and Christians are together in the same trenches resisting the imposition of an ideology upon both our houses by the U.S.A.

Hezbollah is not on a collision course with the people of America. We hold great esteem for the American people. We are shocked by the interference the American government puts in the way of dialogue with the American people.

We want you to know that we honor both Jesus and Mary in our land. Mary is revered in every household as the mother of Jesus. As you know Jesus Christ is part of our land's spiritual heritage. He walked here. We regard you as people of faith. You are of a church following the teaching of Christ who had to drive out of the temple the money changers. We must not have a small political group the, religious Zionists, with their political religion interfering with conversation. As Hezbollah we welcome you to our land and assure you that we are fully aware of your concern for truth and justice which support your mission.

According to my memory this is most of what the Sheik said, though he had a few more phrases denouncing U.S. foreign policy early in his remarks. I responded:

May the Peace of God be with you. In the name of Jesus Christ and your prophet Mohammed whom we respect may peace be upon you and your beautiful land.

We are a committee, a group of twenty-four people from the Presbyterian Church U.S.A. whose task it is to listen to you, to learn of your message, and to take our learnings back to the Church so that we can better advise our General Assembly to formulate policy. That policy will be decided upon through a democratic process within our Assembly to guide our church of two and a half million people regarding the Middle East.

Our church is committed to just peacemaking actions (which include human rights, racial justice, peacemaking initiatives, working through the UN, aid for sustainable human development, a preference for non-violent strategies, and other practices). But we do not totally forsake the need for force for self-defense or the defense of others. Let me share with you two Biblical stories that both occurred within a hundred kilometers of this place. The first is from the Hebrew Bible, the Book of II Kings. The King of Damascus wanted to invade Israel. He was thwarted at every turn because the Israel forces knew his intentions. His advisors told him that Elisha the prophet foresaw his plans and informed the King of Israel. So the King of Damascus sent a force to seize Elisha, but this political prophet prayed and the armed forces of Damascus were blinded by God. Elisha then led them into the city of Samaria and they were surrounded. The King of Samaria wanted to put the forces of Damascus to death, but Elisha said, "No, give them a feast." They were restored to sight and they feasted in Samaria. They were then freed to leave. The story concludes the King of Damascus never invaded Israel again. May it be so.

The second story is from Acts in the New Testament. Paul was a religious persecutor as have been many religious leaders. He was present at the death of Stephen. He was on his way to Damascus to persecute Christians when an appearance of the risen Christ confronted him and blinded him. Jesus the Christ accused him of persecuting himself. Paul was ordered to proceed to Damascus where the early Christians feared him, but he gave up the way of violence and by giving up violence he became an Apostle. True religion gives up violence and finds other ways to resolve conflicts. Paul's story needs to be a story for all religion.

We accept the compassionate words from Hezbollah of welcome, esteem, and good wishes. We respect the call to dialogue from Hezbollah.

I want to say that from my own personal experience dialogue with Moslem leaders has been easier than with Jewish leaders. (From my later perspective, I wish I had not said that.)

Because our theology is grounded in the Hebrew prophets we know how difficult it is in this history to achieve peace.

We have heard from you that the American intervention in Lebanon was a disaster, and that it did not contribute to peace. We have heard that resolution 1599 is a sore problem for you. You have told us that sectarian conflicts have been deepened by American interference. We have heard of your hopes for our visit.

As a Church we have said clearly that the occupation of the West Bank must be ended. We have criticized the invasion of Iraq as "Immoral, unwise, and illegal." We are a church of great economic power and political influence and we are trying to use that power to influence the American people.

Let me conclude, so that the dialogue can begin, with a few points of things that make for peace:

1. Without peace among the religions there is no chance for world peace.
2. It is difficult to achieve peace, but social work, education, toleration, and good government all contribute to the realities of society that provide a chance for peace.

In conclusion our church has and will struggle for aid for human development, resistance to militarism, and support of institutions of international order that can limit national power and reduce any nation's attempt to control other nations.

Peace be with you and may the conversation continue.

Another forty-five minutes of discussion through translators continued. Much of it was on the theological understanding of the relationship of forgiveness to justice. Human rights was extensively discussed in this context; animal rights were mentioned by the Sheik. In Stone's response to the Sheik he emphasized that in Christian perspective God's grace and forgiveness preceded the achievement of justice, enriched it, and followed the incompleteness of justice. A question about U.S. elections prompted the Sheik to suggest that vis-à-vis the Middle East there was not much of a choice, but that he hoped American Christians would read the Gospels, look into their hearts, and follow Jesus.

Hezbollah participated at the time of our visit in the Lebanese Parliament and governed Southern Lebanon where six of our churches are located. On entering Southern Lebanon we passed beyond the Lebanon government's control as we cleared the Army's checkpoint. On clearing the Hezbollah checkpoint our safety depended on Hezbollah; throughout the trip, they provided a unarmed military escort. Along the border we were sometimes between Israeli and Hezbollah border posts, but we felt no insecurity as Presbyterians on a peacemaking trip. Furthermore the trip carried with it several of the Presbyterian experts on peacemaking and the Middle East. Mr. John J. Detterick, Executive Director of the General Assembly Council of the Presbyterian Church U.S.A., had appointed a six-member project team on the Middle East and half of them were traveling with us. We had no idea at the time of how this would play out, and certainly we were completely unaware of how church leadership would respond to this visit which they had sponsored.

I had written on Shiite terrorism in 1984 arguing for armed guards on American Middle Eastern airplane flights and condemning the U.S. practice of inadequately protecting U.S. Marines in Lebanon. Since that time I had written again on militant Islamic terrorism and al Qaeda in particular in *Church and Society*, an official Presbyterian journal. Everyone who had read my essay or the report of the task force on terrorism to the General Assembly which I chaired understood I advocated a Christian realist approach to respond to terrorist acts. This approach uses soft diplomacy of correcting offensive U.S. policies where possible, interreligious dialogue, respectful diplomacy, humanitarian and development aid, multilateral cooperation, and so on. It also affirms suppression and punishment of those who commit terrorist acts. It prefers international legal means, but it also recognizes the need for the use of national military force for the protection of the nation. No nation-state can be expected to passively accept terrorist acts that murder its citizens. A nation must also be careful to observe just war criteria and international law standards in its use of military force, even in self-defense.

So I, after refusing twice, reluctantly agreed to speak to Hezbollah. Previous dialogue sessions with Moslems in India, Kashmir, Israel, the West Bank, Pittsburgh Theological Seminary, and East Liberty Presbyterian Church all had ambiguous results and no more was expected from this encounter. But as a Christian, you try to accept responsibilities the Church asks you to undertake, and the practices of just peacemaking include taking some risks in initiating peacemaking actions. Our whole trip from dialogue with the Sheik at Kahim Detention Center to conversation with the Grand Imam in Cairo was such an initiative.

The next day in Beirut, we learned that our visit had become a Middle East media event. Our wide-ranging discussion of an hour and a half about forgiveness, justice and politics, terrorism, peacemaking, divestment, and social change was edited down to a sound bite. Hezbollah TV produced a one-minute bite of the Sheik condemning President Bush's foreign policy in the Middle East, the war in Iraq, and American policy vis-à-vis Lebanon and two sentences of mine thanking the Sheik for his generous greeting of our church committee and the aside to him of finding it personally easier to dialogue with Moslem leaders than Jewish leaders in the present situation. Al Jazeera broadcast the sound bite over the Middle East. A variety of Arab and English newspapers also printed different accounts. Generally the newspaper versions were more fulsome and accurate and they omitted the sentences that caused so much uproar in the United States.

The Al Jazeera interpretation found its way through CNN to the United States Those familiar with the Middle East know that local newspapers and television there are politically controlled serving national or partisan purposes. Hundreds of complaints about our visit to the South of Lebanon were received at Church headquarters and the Church executives responded. They claimed we were told not to go to South Lebanon and the words reported were "Reprehensible." On returning to the United States two of the Church executives on the trip were fired. Various Church executive who had only Al Jazeera's interpretation of the meeting and who had no idea what was actually said had the Moderator of the Church demand the resignation of two of the committee members on the trip.

We understood the long-standing practice (both religious and secular) of trying to hush turmoil by resignations and firings. But this entire storm was basically a media event caused by Arab propaganda and Christian overreaction. The government of Israel cancelled official meetings with our group so we met with non-governmental Israelis. While our church leadership was denouncing us, we continued our trip meeting presidents, non-governmental peace organizations, the Jordanian advisor to the King, the Grand Imam, academic leaders, refugees, rabbis, civil rights activists, churches, social welfare workers, Moslem/Christian dialogue leaders, missionaries, Jews, children in a refugee camp, and a former hostage of Hezbollah.

Before interviewing me a local newspaper urged that I be stoned and kicked into the gutter. At that point, though the newspaper had not phoned me, it was reported that it phoned both the government and the Church urging my arrest or disciplinary action. While we are all suspicious of Middle East reporting, no newspaper source in the Middle East had been so prejudicial. The *Tribune Review* editorial attributed statements never said, and at the time of publication it had little idea of what had been said. A follow-up interview, after the damage had been done and strangers from Pittsburgh were attacking me, corrected some of the misperceptions. But they also secured a rabbi, unknown to me to comment on the interview, and to dismiss me as naive.

An anonymous letter from Brooklyn to the Church headquarters threatened arson to Presbyterian churches. The threat was to bomb them while they were full of worshippers unless the Presbyterian Church changed its policy toward Israel. Charles Reynolds, a Presbyterian minister, commented: "If they think our churches are full, they don't know our churches." The writer of the letter was later arrested.

So while those seeking more justice for the Palestinians, including Jews, Christians, and Moslems, supported the visit, others found it a dreadful mistake. Church officials supporting pressure on Israel to moderate its position through selective/phased divestment policies were subjected to severe pressures, and their attempts at dialogue with Jewish leaders were rendered even more difficult.

The Advisory Committee on Social Witness Policy apologized to Church leadership for the pain and difficulties caused by the broadcasts of the visit to Hezbollah, and they acknowledged that given the religious and political tensions within the United States it had been unwise. The Moderator, Executive Director, and Stated Clerk have acknowledged that their letter concerning the visit was hurtful and they have said they were sorry for the pain they caused. Both groups pledged to work together on policy issues pursuing peace and justice in the Middle East and to conduct a full and fair review of the firing of the coordinator of the Advisory Committee. The executive committee of the General Assembly Committee approved the procedures of the Executive Director in firing the two executives who shared leadership for the trip with many others in the church bureaucracy. Others who planned the details of the trip including the visit to Hezbollah continued in office. In over forty years of travel, often to controversial groups (Soviet officials, Cuban Communists, Eastern European Communists, Liberation Movements) I had never seen a study trip as productive of sustained conversations with philosophers, organizers, presidents, rabbis, priests, ministers, foreign ministers, imams, refugees, church members, members of parliament, peace activists, and militants as on this study trip. The attempt to meet with people perceived as terrorists by the U.S. government in an effort to understand and speak with them was in this case and this time too threatening to the Church for it to be supported in a time of conflict. Visits by other churches to the same group are sometimes under the screen of the media. The pain in the Presbyterian Church may necessitate that for the immediate future at least conversations with controversial groups must be handled with more care. Then the learnings from dialogue can inform the Church.

Peter Sulyok's question in Chicago over what I should say to President Arafat was answered by a phone call to our van while we traveled to his compound in Ramallah. The Chairman Arafat regretted to inform us that he was too ill to receive us, but he hoped for a visit in the future. Peace, after Arafat's death, will require a lot of conversations with various groups. It is to be wished that the United States government and nongovernmental agencies can play the role of honest mediator in these talks toward whatever peace can be sustained in the region. Movement toward peace will require that Moslems, Christians, Jews, and secular people talk with a lot of people with whom they disagree. Many of those talked with on all sides will have taken lives in combat or have even taken civilian lives. This is the nature of the conflict which involves very few major players who are innocent. I hope that the dialogue participants and negotiators can increasingly find their common religious grounds in peacemaking and not war making. Two years after the visit, some U.S. leaders in international affairs are suggesting we should include enemies like Iran and Syria in dialogue about the occupation of Iraq. Israel has invaded Lebanon with U.S. support, destroyed villages, fought with Hezbollah, and withdrawn. Media propaganda during the invasion pretty consistently referred to the inhabitants of Southern Lebanon and Hezbollah as our enemies. I was in Rome in the summer of 2006 when the U.S. Secretary of State, hurriedly assembled foreign ministers from Europe there to disengage Israel from Lebanon. The United States supported Israel's attack with weapons (including anti-personnel cluster bombs) and diplomatic support until it appeared to be slowing down and accomplishing nothing but destroying villages and Lebanese citizens. As usual in modern war most of the victims were children and women. No major U.S. leader suggested talking with Hezbollah. Awareness of the United States' own religious traditions will sometime in the future incline Americans to dialogue with this religious/political paramilitary party in southern Lebanon, the Baka Valley, and south Beirut. When such a dialogue, striving to lay the groundwork for peace occurs, I pray that the church which condemned our dialogue without knowing what was said and the newspapers that vilified us will be supportive of conversation even with those they regard as enemies. Perhaps then the coordinator of the trip, who was dismissed from his church position presumtively, will be honored as a precursor of many who have taken the aspirations of Hezbollah into account in these conflicts. The arrogance of the American leadership which refuses to talk with Hamas, the elected government of Palestine and the de facto ruler of Gaza, is startling. American citizens will need to lead the government into these conversations. Americans should not forget there was a time when the U.S. policy was not to have diplomatic relations or dialogue with China. The isolation of Cuba failed. Realism requires recognition and conversation with perceived enemies.

Thoughts About the Land After a Dialogue with a Chicago Settler in Efrat

Trips to Israel may not be sufficient to give one a perspective on the land. But in a world where billions of dollars are sent to Israel by the U.S. government to secure the land, billions to Egypt to secure the military cooperation with Israel, and hundreds of millions to support displaced Palestinians by politicians who have never visited the Middle East, several visits are better than none. In a militarized suburb of Jerusalem the settler from Chicago assured a visiting group that God had given the land to the Jews. His automatic weapons assured God's gift of the unarmed Palestinians' land. In a Palestinian village, I talked with a father whose ten-year-old daughter had been shot as she left a shop with her after-school treat across the street from her school. The girl's death, the settler's religious belief, and U.S. military aid and policy are all parts of the same occupation.

The Hebrew Scripture of the Christian Old Testament are about God and the land. Christians spiritualize these scriptures, but they really are about the religious claims to occupation of the land. The Jewish claim to this land whether by secular or religious Jews is still grounded in the narrative of God's giving the land to the descendents of Abraham. Both Jews and Moslems regard themselves as Abraham's heirs. A critical reading of these scriptures unveils the legitimatization process of the taking of these lands by the Hebrews. It is true that the Christian Bible neither begins with Hebrews in the land of Israel/Palestine nor ends with Jews in control of the land. Still between Abraham who lives as an alien among the Canaanites (Genesis 12:5 and 17:8) and Hittites (Genesis 23:4) whom he recognizes as owning the land and the final times of Revelation with the Romans as occupiers there is a lot about Hebrew occupation and exile from the land. Hebrew sovereignty from Saul to Zedekiah is relatively undistinguished with a sorry lot of kings, excepting David who held the country together, recognizing dominance from Egypt, Assyria, Babylon, and Persia, but still the line from 1000 to 587 B.C.E. is a considerable period even if the land is shared with others: Canaanites, Philistines, Hittites, Samaritans, and so forth. After Persian and Greek rule there is the brief period of Hasmonean rule under Hebrew sovereignty until the Roman annexation of Judea.

Walter Brueggemann[3] provided an interpretation to support a Biblical theology of God's gift of the land to the landless Hebrews. There is very little in Brueggemann's biblical theology that would give pause to extreme Christian Zionists or the Jewish Chicago settler in claiming that God had given the land to the Hebrews. Even some recognition that Hebrews had written a religious legitimatization for their despoiling of the original inhabitants in the conquest times (ca. 1200 B.C.E.) and that it is still used in modern times of the twenty-first-century Palestinians would have helped. His quickly written conclusion, with easy generalizations about Marxist-Christian dialogue and theologians speaking for the disposed, neglects the presently disposed Palestinians. After nearly two hundred pages of God giving the land to the Jews the most he can muster for the people who lost the land was: "While the Arabs surely have rights and legitimate grievances, the Jewish people are peculiarly the pained voice of the land in the history of humanity, grieved Rachel weeping." (Jer. 31:15)[4]

His book's theme of God giving the land to the Hebrews is unequivocal and neglectful of the people who lost the land. Such naivete sounds the death knell for his form of biblical theology among critical readers or those sympathetic to the suffering of those dispossessed by conquest.

"Land is a central if not the central theme of Biblical faith."

"The Bible is the story of God's people with God's land."

"Israel's involvement is always with land and with Yahweh."

"Israel is to have the buoyant conviction that creatures of the word can in any circumstance trust the word that will destroy all its enemies."[5]

Brueggemann's argument to carry the centrality of the Old Testament land into the New Testament is less persuasive than his Old Testament study. In the New Testament all of the main characters are landless, and the Roman occupiers of the land are not central to the story. He establishes his main point that the land is a major theme of Hebrew religion; where he fails is not recognizing the other sides of the narrative. The Canaanites and the Palestinians had theologies, too, and among Palestinian Christians the roots go back to landless disciples of Jesus the Christ. What Brueggemann in this book presents as a gift of God was historically a series of battles which gradually conquered the land, deposing and killing others of God's children. Without more emphasis upon the Hebrew ideological writing of scripture one is left with an affirmation of Hebrew Holy War to seize the land as the main consequence of the Bible. This is little better than legitimatizing Palestinian jihad to practice terrorism against civilians in defense of the Moslem homeland. Both Brueggemann and Bush's crusades must be avoided. Another Presbyterian scholar of the Old Testament has written a much more moderate book on the land. Interestingly he was educated in the same graduate institution as Brueggemann and by some of the same scholars. W. Eugene March's *God's Land on Loan*[6] does not separate God from the human struggles over the land, but he sees the diving requirements of peace and justice as more central to the Biblical narrative than the ownership of the land. The earth is the Lord's and humans are only tenants on it. Many different people have lived on the land of Palestine and controlled its resources. Biblical Israel is radically different from the contemporary historical Israel, and historical promises in the Hebrew Bible were either fulfilled in their time or are religious hopes by the Hebrew people for the end of time. They are not to govern politics in the twenty-first century. March works as a theologian and refuses to be blinded by a literal application of ancient Hebrew history and its reading of its conflicts into demands for today's political compromises achieved through a multitude of contending forces. God's work in history for March has brought Christians, Jews, and Moslems into Palestine, and the human task is under God's guidance to achieve as much justice and fair stewardship of the gift of the land as possible. The compromises for peace that both Jews and Moslems want will be found in recognizing that God is holy and that the land is not. The land can be compromised and a political solution achieved while still holding to the absolute devotion to their respective perspectives n the divine. The confusion of the land with God will only make compromise and peace impossible. March seems to me to have a helpful mixture of biblical insight, theological perspective, and political realism to avoid the dangers of absolutism which encourage fanaticism. His perspective starts where the responsive ethic discussed in the first chapter concluded with the priority of "What is going on?" The historical reality is first considered then for him the Biblical perspectives and theological perspectives are used in conjunction with modern social science.

The first time I lived in Israel, I lived among scholars who said little of direct relevance to the struggles going on over the olive orchards lying outside our walled compound. The second time, I traveled with an official delegation meeting heads of state, foreign ministers, and religious dignitaries and the citizens were crowded masses in growing Arab cities. On the third trip I visited more refugee camps, talked with more nongovernmental organization representatives, and saw more suffering among Palestinians than before. A new hermeneutical paradigm or model of interpretation emerged from my interpretation of our discontent with American support for Israeli occupation.

Israel's separation of Gaza from the sea, air, and the bordering land unless convenient to Israel reduces Gaza to the conditions of a North American nineteenth-century Indian reservation. When European North Americans stopped killing Native Americans they confined them to reservations where they could not practice their native hunting habits. Confinement, disease, and oppression reduced their population to near insignificance. Gaza is dependent upon Israel and formerly on Egypt; denial of access ruins the lives of the people.

The European conquest of North America was done in the name of God almost as much as the taking of this land by the Hebrews. A letter of a homesteading great-grandfather in Iowa in the 1850s even refers to the Dakota (Sioux) as Philistines. Sometimes selected Indians were paid for European rights to the land, but there was no official ownership of the land by those who sold it as it was communal hunting land. Without game to hunt the natives starved. Policy from Washington was to permit settlers to take the game and leave the hunting land unfit for Indian inhabitation. When war was made upon Indians reluctant to surrender their land, crops were destroyed and homes and villages burned. Treaty after treaty was made pushing the natives always further west so one tribe fell upon another's land. Resistance to superior numbers and armaments was futile though often undertaken. It really made little difference whether resistance was nonviolent or violent as the land was taken anyway and without regard to the Indians' belief system as the white system was privileged by power. The Dakota would say, "They never have enough." Basically each European wanted his own farm; collectively they wanted all of the land. The meaning of the Indians was broken by taking the land, killing the animals, disregarding Indian honor and ethos, and confining survivors of disease and persecution to the reservations.

The wall and road system built on the Palestinian territory cuts the shepherd from his pastures, the olive farmers from their fields, patients from hospitals, children from schools, while assuring Israel of the control of the best farm land and the water aquifers. The Palestinians have been broken during the period of the Oslo peace process into separated cantons or Bantustans which are not viable for a good life.[7] Daily Palestinians may be humiliated and resistance may lead to death. There is no way for Palestinians to govern or plan for they are at the mercy of arbitrary decisions by the occupying power supported by the U.S. power. They, even today, do not know where Israel intends to conclude its borders. It seems, as it did to the Sioux, that the Europeans always want more.

Palestinian resistance has largely been through the pursuit of legal redress or nonviolent petitions, demonstrations, appeals, and so forth. Rock-throwing escapades have been ridiculous and counterproductive. Terrorist activity on the part of Palestinians has been immoral and counterproductive as Israel has responded disproportionately with its own terror. Israeli suppression through terror in the form of intimidation, torture, imprisonment, assassination, and warfare is also immoral. Casualties in conflicts between Palestinians and Israelis result in deaths of about four Palestinians to one Israeli with most casualties on both sides consisting of civilians including outrageous numbers of children. Both occupying governance and resistance to occupying governance usually involve some terrorism. Terrorism thrives most notably among occupied suppressed populations. But attacks on civilians remain immoral and are rightly condemned by religious morality and international law.

The paradigm of European conquest of North America holds little hope for Palestinians as a nation. Some Europeans did defend Native Americans, some evangelized them, some taught agriculture and other Western forms of life, and some Native Americans survived on welfare from their conquerors.

But basically they were destroyed, only to somewhat recover through population growth in the succeeding century.

Another more hopeful paradigm is suggested by President Jimmy Carter's new book *Palestine: Peace Not Apartheid*.[8] Apartheid was overcome partially through local resistance and partially through international economic pressure. So the Israeli taking of Palestinian land through despoiling of population, the Jewish settlement expansions, the wall, confiscation policies, and denial of Palestinians the right to build homes through a ruinous policy of "permit" policy requires international economic pressure as well as the internal resistance of the Palestinians. A goal of 1967 borders with compensation for Palestinians deplaced before 1967 with a shared Jerusalem is neither anti-Israeli nor anti-Semitic. It is a way of moving towards an Arab-Israel peace supported by the United States that can hold and help restore security in the region. The divided and broken Palestinian-Gaza government is obviously unequipped to negotiate a settlement with Israel. The U.S. government is incapable of moving toward more just peace in Palestine/Israel for the near future. So, nongovernmental organizations and communities of conscience including churches, will have to move one by one, with both their own funds and interpretations to disengage from powers which support Israel's current oppression or in any way support the forces that kill Israeli citizens. While both Palestinian and Israeli fears can be understood given their histories, neither of their murders of civilians can be approved by forces working and hoping for peace. Then, even our Jewish settler from Chicago can have his question answered. He thinks he knows that God gave Israel the land; he just did not know exactly how much God gave away. The answer is the 67 borders with a shared Jerusalem and no more. Such a tough-minded approach will require strategies to counter pressure from pro-Israeli forces that want to see Israel expand. Churches attempting to manage their own investments responsively for the long-range health of Israel and the church's own integrity have felt the pressure as will groups that support policy to discourage Israel's expansion and Palestinian reduction in the future.

Beyond the compromises needed for an Israel-Palestine settlement are the issues of the clash of militants from Islam and militants from Christianity. President Carter's focus demands an expansion into the history of Islam-Christian relations and the immediate issues of empire and democracy.

Notes

1. Jimmy Carter, who disparages the U.S. reluctance to dialogue with enemies, only mentions the need to initiate dialogue with government leaders in Damascus

and the Palestinian government of Mahmoud Abbas. *Palestine: Peace Not Aparthied* (New York: Simon and Schuster, 2006), 203.

2. The best discussion of Hezbollah I know of in a church publication is found in the fine issue of *Church and Society* edited by Vernon Broyles (July/August, 2006) where several short essays by experts from the Middle East discuss the party, 116–31.

3. Walter Brueggemann, *The Land* (Philadephia: Fortress Press, 1977).

4. *Ibid.*, 190.

5. *Ibid.*, 3, 13, 52, 70.

6. W. Eugene March, *God's Land on Loan: Israel Palestine and the World* (Louisville: Westminster John Knox Press, 2007).

7. Zbigniew Brzezinski, *Second Chance*, (New York: Basic Books, 2007), 124.

8. Jimmy Carter, *Palestine: Peace Not Apartheid.*

CHAPTER SIX

~

War and Wisdom from Islam and Christianity

A small circle of followers formed around Mohammed, believing his vision. They were persecuted and harassed. The city of Media invited him to resolve political disputes, and he became the leader of the city in A.D. 622, marking the beginning of Islam. From its beginning Islam was a religious-political movement settled in a community and embracing the world. Before his death, through a series of battles he prevailed over Mecca. In the struggle the early alliance with Judaism came to an end and the Jews were expelled from Medina. He gave God the credit for the reception in Mecca of his leadership and for the new religion. Mohammed, first a prophet, was also an organizer, a warrior claiming all of life for Islam or submission to Allah.

The next few years saw Islam spread across Arabia, Syria, Palestine, Egypt, Iraq, and Persia and internal rivalries for the succession to the prophet produced plots, coups, counterplots, and assassinations. The struggles produced rifts in the growing empire which continue to the present day, breaking the ideal of the one united Islamic community.

The assassination of Ali cleared the way for the Umayyad dynasty which moved the capitol to Damascus and away from the more austere life of Medina and the semi-nomadic life of Kufah. The dynasty's defeat of Ali's family at Karbala in 689 set the stage for unknowing America's drift into the Sunni-Shia civil war in Iraq in 2006. From the defeat came themes of martyrdom, suffering for the faith, passion plays, and the potent political-religious symbols and actions which Americans were unprepared to comprehend when they took up the burden of invading the Islamic homeland for the restoration of the Kuwait monarchy, oil revenue, mistaken ideas about weapons, terrorism, and Iraq national policy.

The tragedy of America in Iraq, of course, is also the story of neoconservative imperialism, American fundamentalism, mistaken intelligence, and ignorance. But from a historical perspective it is but another chapter in the long war between Europeans and Middle Eastern Moslems. Already before the martyrdom of Hussain, Christians had lost several of their cities as had the Persian Zoroastrians. By A.D. 711 Islamic fleets were controlling the Mediterranean and conquering former Christian provinces.

The dynasty from Persia, the Abbasids, moved the capital out of Arab lands to Baghdad and made it the center of an empire composed of many nationalities. The knowledge and art of these cultures were absorbed and transformed even as the Abbasid political competence declined and the empire fractured. Spain, Egypt, and Baghdad all emerged as separate centers of Islamic culture and power.

The conquest of Europe was stopped by Charles Martel at the battle of Tours in France in A.D. 732. The counterthrusts of Europe's Crusades into Palestine occupied over a hundred years but were turned back when much of Islam was united politically by Saladin. The Moslem conquest of central Asia was more successful being completed by 752. The Chinese resisted Islam even into the modern period, and conflicts between Chinese Moslems and the central government were not uncommon.

By the fourteenth century most of northern India had been conquered by armies coming through the Kyber Pass. The role would extend until the British conquest in the nineteenth century and then the division into Pakistan and India in 1947 leaving India with the largest Moslem population outside of Indonesia. The Indian subcontinent was the scene of various European clashes from the sixteenth century through the twentieth century as Dutch, Portuguese, French, and finally the British Empire had their try at India. Islamic loyalty was insufficient to hold Bangladesh and Pakistan together.

In Indonesia, the Dutch would wrest political sovereignty from Moslem control while Spain under the Hapsburgs fought Moslems in Vienna in the seventeenth century after expelling Moslems and Jews from Spain in 1492. The Moslems in the Turkish form finally conquered Constantinople in 1453 and subjected the Balkans to Moslem rule until the modern period.

Though European empire builders assaulted the hinterlands of Islamic power from the sixteenth through the nineteenth century, it was really the twentieth century that realized the rise of the West and the subjection of the heartland of Islam. The defeat of the Ottoman Empire in 1918 finished the dismantling of European Islamic rule except for the territory around Istanbul.

Yugoslavia, Greece, Romania, and Bulgaria were all restored to Christian rule. Iraq, Jordan, Palestine, and Syria were all reduced to European protectorates or colonies. Iran and the Gulf states were dominated by Britain. The United States got control of a majority of Kuwait's oil and of the whole only Arabia had real sovereignty after World War I. All of the great former Islamic centers of Cordova, Cairo, Damascus, and Baghdad were governed by Europeans of at least nominal Christian faith, but, of course, they had been controlled by Christians before the conquests of Islam in the one hundred years after Mohammed. Also all of the Moslem lands of Africa were reduced to European colonies, mostly French.

To a very real degree the jihads of Islam never ended, they were only defeated. Also the counterattacks by Europeans, sometimes called Crusades, never ended either. The wars between Christian Moscow and Moslems were ended only by the conquests of Russia and resumed after the 1991 failure of the Soviet state. Gradually the European colonies dissolved or were overthrown after World War II, but the establishment of Israel in 1948 by the United Nations was a counterthrust. Israel, England, and France invaded Egypt in 1956. The United States and France tried to determine Lebanon's direction in the 1980s. The failed Serbian wars of the 1990s were to some Serbs crusades and to some Moslems, jihads. The United States built bases around the Persian Gulf and armed many states including especially Israel. The United States defeated Iraq in 1991, and invaded and conquered and occupied Afghanistan in 2001 and Iraq in 2003.

Through the shifts in power created by World War II, the United States has to a large degree assumed the roles played by Great Britain east of Suez since 1956. The U.S. ambiguity about its imperial role does not permit it to bear this burden gladly. In the long run of history the future of boys from New York and Iowa trying to dominate Baghdad and Kabul is not promising. An argument can be made that after the Cold War America's armed forces no more belong east of Suez than did Great Britain's.

Moslem motives for the conquest of Christian lands were no more noble than Christian motives to reconquer those lands or to seize sovereignty from Moslems. In both cases motives of mission, money, and management can be seen. In the light of continual conflict interrupted by periods of peace, truce, stalemate, and exhaustion a Moslem's writer's conclusion to his history of Islam seems appropriate.

> To begin with, Muslims must deal with the modern world, not through confrontation and conflict, but through diplomacy and patient dialogue. . . . It may be further argued that throughout Muslim history, diplomacy and dialogue

produced far better results in resolving conflicts and achieving peace than did military power and conquest.[1]

The majority of Moslems live within parliamentary governments, even if in the Arabian world monarchs, dictators, and sheiks seem the predominant forms of governing power. The liberalism of parliamentary government, non-patriarchal forms of culture, and industrialization did not emerge out of Islam. Such expressions of Western values clash with traditional Arab Moslem culture, and can disrupt Arab identity. The problem of identity confusion is increased when the United States supports traditional dictators and monarchs for economic or geographical considerations. U.S. military invasion into heartlands of Islamic culture, even in support of some Arabs, disrupts Arab identity even further. In retrospect it is not anomalous that some Arabs strive to strike back at the United States.

During the reign of Saddam Hussein, mistakes by both U.S. diplomats and Hussein's judgment led to two wars by the Presidents Bush and to Hussein's execution. Hussein's risk at invading Kuwait was met by U.S. imperial interests supported by the majority of the nations of the world to throw Iraq's armies back. Mistakes again by the United States fueled now by neoconservative exaggerated imperial oil interests led to the second war, squandering the support for the United States in Afghanistan against Osama bin Laden. None of the parties to the conflict are motivated solely by religion, all of the parties use religion and several of the parties including the United States are partially motivated by religious ideologies and grandiose illusions of empire.

Even given the long history of war between Islamic countries and Christian countries this conflict in Iraq has some special conceptual features. Two of these concepts are empire and democracy, and our analytic journey turns toward these concepts in the American philosopher of politics and religion, Reinhold Niebuhr.

The Concept of Empire

Niebuhr regarded the United States of America as an empire. His last major writing on the subject, *The Structure of Nations and Empires*, was published in 1959 before the collapse of the Soviet Union. So he was not required to ask whether the United States was a world empire. Of course it has never been a requirement of the term *empire* that it encompass world sovereignty. The Roman Empire was mostly a European and Mediterranean venture. It coexisted with the Chinese Empire and the Persian Empire. The Dutch Empire coexisted with the Spanish, French, English, Chinese, and Russian empires. Many biblical empires were relatively small. At times Mexico and Brazil have assumed the mantle of empire. Canada which is much larger geographically than most empires is not usually referred to as an empire, but it does include different nations. Like many writers on empire, Niebuhr's definition is not very strict, for after all, ancient patterns of dominion have both similarities and many differences from contemporary patterns. He expresses it in a question:

The question remains whether there is a recurring pattern of empire in history in

> [T]he sense that strong nations exercise authority over weaker nations; and whether such authority is compounded inevitably in the present as it has been in the past, of both force and presitige.[2]

His study was a Cold War study and even the names he lists in the preface reflect that reality: J. Robert Oppenheimer, George Kennan, Hans J. Morgenthau, John C. Bennett, Kenneth Thompson, Arthur Schlessinger, Jr., and Llwellyn Woodward. Its central purpose was to analyze the ideological and power factors in the competition between two empires, one fueled by liberal democratic thought and one by utopian Marxian thought. He regarded the American empire as at some disadvantage in the Asian and African worlds where many countries asserted their independence of American influence by their votes at the United Nations and in encouraging socialist tendencies that sometimes reflected Soviet influence.

In Niebuhr's perspective empires evolved out of powerful city-states and the nation-states historically followed patterns of decline of empires. He recognized that empire as a term was criticized by both Marxists and liberals. But as a leader of alliances against the Russian Empire embodied in the Soviet Union and the Warsaw Pact nations it was appropriate to regard the United States as an empire. I think for Niebuhr the transcontinental expansion of the United States by the destruction of the Native American nations and the supplanting of the Spanish, French, English, Russian, and Mexican empires with American sovereignty was sufficient to regard the United States as an empire. Empires like other forms of political organization, be they families, tribes, city-states, alliances, or nation-states, are morally ambiguous. He would not condemn a form of organization just because it was large. Imperial policies producing empires are in his mind due to moral, religious, even missionary factors, as well as economic motivations, and finally the motivations of pride and seeking of prestige must be considered. He did not expect to see empires as a form of organization disappear, though some would collapse or divide or be conquered. Like nation-states they come and go and evolve.

None are totally evil and certainly none are entirely good, though in terms of human rights, norms of equality and freedom, and efficient economic institutions some may be better or worse than others.

Christianity and Empire

Christianity is a religion of the Roman Empire. It originated in a province of the Empire, but even more important it was given its definitive shape after the Empire absorbed Christianity. The Islamic nations were created out of their conquests of the dying Roman Empire in the Middle East and Africa. The father of the restorer of the Empire, Charlemagne, defeated the Moslem armies at Tours and saved Europe for Christianity. Even today the classic expressions of Christianity reflect their origins in the predecessor religions of the Empire. It was with great interest, I took up Charles Cochrane's *Christianity and Classical Culture*[4] while staying in Rome. The book had been given to me by Christopher Niebuhr. It had been one of Reinhold Niebuhr's most important books and it still contained his markings and comments. I had read it at Union Seminary forty years ago, but now I read it beside the Roman Forum and in the context of some wanting to expand the American Empire. The sirens of the motorcades of Condoleezza Rice's emergency meeting seeking help to end the Israel invasion of Lebanon filled the air with more noise than the usual bustling crowds of the Via Venetto. Her hurriedly called meeting of foreign ministers in Rome reinforced the sense of some continuity between the Roman Empire and the American Empire. Niebuhr had learned a lot from Cochrane, and some of it he had managed to pass on to me. Forty years earlier in his retirement he had lived out his form of the aphorism that "Education is a log with a teacher on one end and a student on the other," by walking with me each Friday afternoon as I studied religious ethics and international politics at Columbia University. He would, on the one hand, tell stories, and, on the other, probe all of my assumptions, even if they had come from him. He was a master dialectician, even if I was only an academic sponge. I treasured those walks and the seminars in Christian social ethics in which I assisted him for three years. A few years later, in 1971, my son saw me weep for the first time on learning of his death. Niebuhr had written me a couple of months earlier supporting our sojourn in the Washington, D.C., jail in protest against Richard Nixon's war policy.

Through my forty years of teaching I continued to learn from him and to share his perspective on Christian social ethics with students in a variety of colleges, universities, and seminaries. He was just so much better than the alternatives of linguistic analysis, process theology, contextualism, virtue ethics, liberation theology, death of God theology, secular theology, or deconstructionism that came along for their short periods of dominance that one could continue to explore his thought. The loyalty to a tradition was sometimes rewarded and sometimes criticized, but it persisted. Arthur Schlessinger, Jr., and I spoke at the memorial service for him at Riverside Church in 1971. Schlessinger continued to think his own thoughts while confessing his continuing debt to Reinhold Niebuhr. At the 2005 Union Theological Seminary's consultation on Niebuhr we both stressed the complexity of Niebuhr's mind and argued against the overtheologizing of his or any politics. The traditions of political thought have their own autonomy and religion has its own sources, even though they often interact.

Cochrane's book analyzes the relationship of culture and Christianity. It is the story of how pagan religions nourished the Roman Empire until it became exhausted. Then Constantine and Theodosius attempted to practically supplant paganism with a civil version of Christianity. It concludes with Augustine thinking through a militant form of Christianity which could renew culture and fight the demonic in the culture or in the church. Augustine understood the difference between the City of God and the city of earth so he was free to find happiness in the City of God. He sought the rule of God while hoping for the eschatological fulfillment in the life beyond.

Cochrane knew and affirmed a presupposition of Reinhold Niebuhr about the necessary symbolism of religion when he wrote of Augustine:

> Thus any attempt to describe the operation *Dei* involves the use of symbols which, strictly speaking are metaphorical. In using such symbols, Augustine does so with the full consciousness that they are metaphors.[5]

The symbolism of theological language is most clearly expressed by Niebuhr in the two opening essays of *Faith and Politics*.[6] Reading Cochrane in Rome places one in a full context of religious and political struggle where all of the interesting language is symbolic and attempts at simplistic or literal language are stupid. The symbols of dead gods are all around you in Rome and its outposts of empire scattered around the Mediterranean Sea. The stories of political illusions and vicious attacks upon statesmen by short-lived victors fill one's mind in walks in the Forum or in Vatican City. Foremost in reading Cochrane's tale of politics and religion from Emperor Augustus to theologian Augustine is how the Caesars turned away from republican institutions to an imperial form of rule. Wars and then the following need to enforce the imperial peace required the surrender of the freedoms of the republic to the requirements of security in an unjust empire.

In the empire, the rich became richer and the poor became more dependent and less vital. The drive for luxury of those with power required the impoverishment and slavery of many of the rest, and the role of the citizen with public power declined. Such a system required security measures, and slave revolts resulted in massive crucifixions. This power politics of inequality would be enforced by Rome because its classical thought, according to Cochrane, could not grasp that "All power cometh from on high."[7] Rome would fall because of the failure of its ideas in Cochrane's exposition. The challenge that emerged with the growth of Christianity was in Cochrane's mind the power of love against the love of power.

Cochrane's work shows up in Niebuhr's deepest discussions of the Roman Empire. It appears in *Nature and Destiny of Man, II* [8] in which, in a note, he refers to *Christianity and Classical Culture* by Charles Cochrane[9]: "This work is a profound analysis of the inadequacies of the classical mind in coming to terms with the unique realities of history, in contrast to nature or reason." It is important again much later in his reflections of the Roman Empire in *The Structure of Nations and Empires*[10] and particularly in Niebuhr's high praise of Cicero as a source for democratic theory which emerged in the seventeenth century.

Charles Brown provided a service to all students of Niebuhr's thought by rescuing Niebuhr's review of Cochrane from the obscurity of the *University of Toronto Quarterly* (1941) in his publication of it in *A Reinhold Niebuhr Reader*.[11] In the review Niebuhr confessed the book had "Given me more pleasure than anything I had read in the past decade." He had read a good deal in the decade of the 1930s and evolved to his own mature position. The position of avoiding overdue dependence upon reason or nature, materialism, or idealism focused in the hidden dialectics of history in which he found his mentor in Augustine. Niebuhr loved the book for its close examination of the role of ideas in shaping history as well as for its historical detail. Cochrane had caught the complexities of Christianity's relation to culture surprisingly well. Niebuhr praised the work as a study in theory and practice which was acute in showing how failures in philosophy affected politics. In his conclusion praising Cochrane's interpretation of Augustine, he suggests modern civilization needed an Augustinian foundation beyond either the traditional Catholic or orthodox Protestant interpretations.

Cochrane's perspective on Christian faith correlated closely with Niebuhr's. They both understood Christian faith as the living of the love commandments to love God and to love the neighbor. They both saw Christianity as a militant force with an eschatological vision. They understood in similar ways the ongoing resistance of the world to renewal. Together, they rejected as naive expectations of social moral progress. Cochrane, a little more than Niebuhr, would use "progressive" to describe the hidden movement of God's purpose in history. Lacking Niebuhr's practical experience in the church his understanding of the church was a little more positive than Niebuhr's.

Niebuhr has marked the margins of the book on at least ninety-five pages of the volumes' 516 pages and added eight references on the inside of the back cover. The book bears evidence of being read and studied thoroughly at the time he was writing *The Nature and Destiny of Man*, and the footnotes of his own book affirms the use of Cochrane in his analysis. Cochrane's purpose beyond the historical study unveiled two points: (1) There were inadequate reasons to regard a revival of classicism as a solution to the Western world's malaise, and (2) Christian criticism of classical ideas established the impossibility of finding security, peace, or virtue "Through political action" or especially through submission to a political leader. Consequently, both Cochrane and Niebuhr's philosophies of history, even if not promising worldly success prove the hopes of the Europeans in Nazism and Fascism to be illusions in their own time.

I read the book in a time different from Cochrane and Niebuhr's time. Fundamentalists, Zionists, anti-science politicians, neoconservatives, social conservatives, and deniers of climate warming and evolution unite to try and impose republican institutions upon Iraq. Cochrane gently reminds us of another religious fanatic, Julian the Apostate, who lost his army of 65,000 and his life in an overextension of *Pax Roma* into Iraq. Our own invasion is such an overextension, and we pray that we will escape at less of a cost. May I be clear, republican politics are better than totalitarian or authoritarian politics, and we should encourage them, but to try to impose them is a mistake in both thought and practice. Profound Christian theology knows how ambiguous politics is and though it may fight a war of defense or a war to destroy al Qaeda, a war to model a Middle Eastern state after ours is a categorical mistake.

When classical political thought was unable to recognize that power was from God, it lost its possibility of criticizing the abuse of power by the rich oligarchy. Even the oligarchs lost the possibility of criticizing the military emperors. As inequality is increased by the role of money in our politics freedom is praised more. But there is no real freedom without balancing equality. The rich receive political access denied to the poor and only dreamed of by the declining middle class. My own experience from teaching Christian social ethics to the managerial class of Americans in Pittsburgh is that they are seldom free to function as critics of their corporations or as free citizens to oppose mistaken wars and unjust tax policies. Is the reduction of the aspirations for equality in American politics the domestic side of imperial politics abroad? I still like to think that Americans can work for the common good and not just for their own welfare. We still have republican institutions which can control the political excesses of money and protect our republic. But the pressures of debt, public and private, threaten a crisis as does the loss of purpose in a mistaken war. We are not threatened by a dictator like Julius Caesar, but we are threatened by imperial pretensions, debt, and an elite which has forgotten that power comes from a God who demands justice. Justice without a larger measure of equality than we have achieved is inadequate and the scales must be rebalanced so that more of our children become the vital, religious, expressive political citizens that we recognize as gifts of God.

But before our children escape the burden of financial debt, the inadequacy of many of our schools, the moral criticism of a world that increasingly finds America repugnant, and costs of mistaken wars, we will have to give up illusions. Niebuhr marked Cochrane's passage on the Christian millennial vision's opposition to dependence on Promethean science or politics:

> "It is a prospect held out to human beings, a prospect for which they are willing to work and fight because it constitutes the fulfillment of their humanity."[12]

A major illusion to be surrendered is American rule in Asia. Our invasions of the Asian mainland do not succeed as we have neither the power nor the intelligence to make them succeed. Those of us who lost our friends in Vietnam do not want to lose our children in Iraq. We have sent expeditionary forces to revolutionary Russia, fought in China, invaded North Korea, bombed Cambodia, lost in Vietnam and Laos, overthrown a government in Iran, garrisoned Saudi Arabia and the Gulf States, and fought two wars in Iraq without sustainable success. We can do business with Asia and pursue those who attack us successfully if we keep focused, and work for good relations with a turbulent Asia without dominating it. Our better future does not rest in trying to remake Asia or pretend we are responsible for its peace. Condoleeza Rice's assertions of making a new Middle East are both silly and an expression of Bush hubris.

Another illusion is that all evil lies outside ourselves. Augustine knew that evil rested in the human will and its corruption. Niebuhr marked Cochrane's note about bad will being rooted in bad love:

> This bad will he defines as the 'will to power' when as he says, "the soul losing its own power relapses from the desire for a common and universal good to one which is individual and private."[13]

The will to power derived from the pride of turning from God gets expressed in ideas that are not totally false and in movements which are not totally wrong. So the efficiency of corporations, capitalism, and the U.S. military can, when not cognizant of the corruption of the will to power and the need for limits, become an evil expression in the world. Our efforts are a mixture of good and evil, and we must make every effort to restrain our evil and to maximize our good. It is very difficult for an army of occupation to maximize the good. It will very likely indulge its supporters and suppliers in corruption. Armies do mistreat occupied civilians, and they torture those suspected of having information. They also torture to humiliate and dominate those who oppose their occupation. Christians who serve a Middle Easterner crucified by a Western power should not expect our occupying army to be a simple blessing to Iraqis, Moslem or Christian.

A young member of Hezbollah from Khiam studying English literature told me of his desire to study Shakespeare in the United States. There is much good in him, even though his comrades may have committed terrorist acts in their defense of Lebanon and in morally indefensible attacks on Israeli citizens. He may have died in an Israeli bombardment paid for by the United States. Laughingly, this twenty year old told me before we went to a worship service in a Presbyterian Church in the south of Lebanon that he wanted to study in the United States, but the U.S. government labeled him a terrorist. We must bring to justice those who attack us, but the religious-social struggle shaking Islam presently has a mixture of good and bad forces in it. How can we expect American adolescents or National Guard troops to sort out the issues between the Shiites and Sunnis which go back thirteen centuries? Can they know what is just when confronted by armed Moslems inside a mosque in the middle of the fight?

Even a machine like a Caterpillar tractor reflects the ambiguity of human life. In the hands of fearful Israelis it becomes an instrument destroying homes, olive and orange groves, and erecting a separation wall. In hands working for the commonwealth of Moslem, Jew, and Christian in the Middle East, it could become a blessing for irrigation works and construction of needed homes and facilities. Categories of evil and good as used by our administration have little meaning, and they represent American failure in theology and politics every time they are uttered to demonize one side in a fifty-year-old conflict. A balanced U.S. policy could gradually receive support in the Middle East, but the U.S. aid programs to Israel and U.S. investment in Israel are not balanced by discontinuing aid to Palestine. Some breaks with one-sided support for Israel's economy and policies will need to be made, not to challenge the security of Israel, but to tame her aggression and to end her occupation of the West Bank.

The above comments are not based on Niebuhr's politics up to his death in 1971. They are governed by the theology that both Cochrane and Niebuhr shared about the dangers of pride and pride of the "will to power." They were formulated in the context of thinking about Roman imperial power near the arch of the victory over Jerusalem by Titus, the crucifixion of Jesus and the slaves, and the loss of a Roman army in Iraq.

Another American illusion is that commerce between nations and democracy bring peace. There may be some benefits for international peace from commerce. It would be a rational assumption that warring with one's trading partners was inefficient. But the United States has participated in wars against most of its major trading partners in its two hundred and two score years of history. Much of U.S. commerce is in weapons and they hardly contribute to peaceful pursuits, but they are used to oppress domestic populations and to trouble neighboring states as well as to deter aggression. U.S. commerce in weapons with Israel and Iraq has done little to stabilize the Middle East. The United States does not usually war with other democracies, though it has subverted their governments and dominated them. In Latin American, elections do not guarantee U.S. noninterference. The wars with Mexico and Canada and Britain have not been recent, however. But U.S. democracy has not restrained the United States from a season of war since World War II. The struggle to force democracy on Iraq leads to civil war, secession by the Kurds, and intervention by Iran, and so far to armed resistance to the United States and democratic governance.

Reading Reinhold Niebuhr on Cochrane in Rome is a strong affirmation of the proximate goals of: promoting international law and cooperation in international initiatives to sustain the environment, human rights, sustainable human development policies, and defense of the United States but not of the whole world. It promotes struggling for social justice in reforming U.S. institutions for the sake of fairness for all children. Affirmation of Christian symbolism of eternal life, resurrection, the Kingdom of God, and judgment of God can all strengthen those who struggle for the above goals. The goals mentioned are already articulated in the social policies of most of the churches. The same reading of the book in Rome, though, warns against decreasing social justice, luxury through privatization, corruption of politics by an oligarchy of money, and imperial risk taking. Concluding this essay while on the Mediterranean Sea reminds one of the costs paid by the world to make it a Roman lake, and that the peace of America does not depend upon it being made an American lake.

In making Christianity the official religion, Theodosius made it a civil religion and a very Roman religion. Christianity as a civil religion sustained itself in a Roman way in the West and held up the empire in the East. Augustine knew that though Christianity had social responsibility it was distinct from the empire. Americans need to learn that very soon, also. The church, in the name of God, needs always to argue for more justice than the civil society will grant. God's will, the nature of the church as a social institution, and the needs of the souls the church nurtures all correlate with the serious struggle for social justice. Cochrane's book shows that the lack of social justice was one of the factors that led to the fall of Rome.

Realism About Democracy

Reinhold Niebuhr's perspective on democracy balanced the illusions of individualism and progress which prompted many to support it with pessimism concerning the finitude and self-interested nature of humanity. During the war with Germany and Japan when there were few democracies still standing, he wrote: "Democracy is a method of finding proximate solutions for insolvable problems."[14] The balance he sought between human possibilities and human realities was expressed in perhaps his most famous aphorism: "Man's capacity for justice makes democracy possible, but man's inclination to injustice makes democracy necessary."[15] He did not argue that democracy was possible everywhere or that it was necessary for all.

Democracy—meaning that the people could meaningfully review government actions and change the governing leaders by a nonviolent process—grew in the Western world and it had depended upon many contingent historical features. It meant much less to Niebuhr than the literal meaning of a people ruling. Politics is always led by the political elite and other oligarchies of the system. Democracy meant that even with all the special interest groups and competing elites there was some process for a majority of the people to reject particular governmental leaders and to exercise a right of review of their policies.

Groups competing for power traditionally exercise power through control of money, military capability, religion, charisma, or ideology. Several factors of historical development were necessary in Niebuhr's analysis to encourage democracy. They included national unity, religious toleration or unity, economic development, literacy and access to information freedom for individual development and expression, and sufficient social justice to gather support for the system. Parliamentary democracy also requires the necessary toughness of the parliamentarians to protect the constitution and the process.[16]

The study of democracy by Niebuhr and Paul Sigmund, *The Democratic Experience: Past and Prospects*, did not find adequate prerequisites for sustainable democracy in many parts of the world. In particular many recently freed colonies did not have adequately balanced social power to ensure the compromises necessary for a parliamentary system to function. Without dispersed social and economic power, military or religious power could overthrow democratic processes. They refused to see democracy as normative for all governments. The historical sources of democracy were in many countries too deficient for democracy to emerge. Niebuhr did not live to see the rush toward democracy after the fall of the Soviet Union. Nor had political science argued in his time that democratic governments promote peace by not fighting among themselves. Yet he saw how parliamentary government could act as a break upon military adventures. Before his death in 1971, he did fear that democratic processes might not be strong enough to contain increasing militarism in the United States, but that was still in the context of the Cold War.

Some democratic processes in many parts of the developing world were subject to interruption by military coups. Also, some societies even without the Western prerequisites like India and Japan were thought to have in their own history factors supporting parliamentary democracy. The analysis of democracy in the Middle East by Niebuhr and Sigmund was pessimistic. Niebuhr could be regarded as an expert on Europe and Sigmund as such on Latin America. Neither, perhaps, possessed expertise on the Middle East.

Niebuhr had taught world religious ethics at Union Theological Seminary for thirty years, but though he covered Buddhist, Hindu, Chinese, Hebrew, Egyptian, Roman, and Greek traditions, his course often omitted Islam. He had never visited the Middle East and his affection for and support of Israel may have blinded him to some positive developments in Islamic political thought. He did not write much about Islam except for eleven pages in *The Democratic Prospect* and about the same in *The Structure of Nations and Empires*. In a chapter "Lessons from Three Empires" he argued that universal religions, Orthodoxy, Catholicism, and Islam, developed versions of absolute religious power which reinforced political claims of particular emperors.

In short, the impulse to dominion on every level, but particularly on the imperial level, is able to use the most varied and contradictory religious impulses and philosophies as instruments of its purposes.[17]

Orthodoxy and Catholicism are among the many subjects of the short chapter on three empires. No Moslem sources are used by Niebuhr in his writing here, and the only documented authority on Islam in the chapter is the 1917 book by Ignaz Goldziher, *Mohammed and Islam*,[18] which is quoted four times. The analysis of Islamic imperialism is very meager and reminiscent of the meager attention given to Islam in the course surveying world religious ethics. His deep Christian support of Zionism was expressed in several essays in *Christianity and Crisis*.

In the Arab world, Niebuhr found weak parliamentary experiments being overcome by military-established dictators who tolerated very little democratic dissent. Even in Turkey, the most successful of the parliamentary systems of the Middle East governments would be deplaced by military government and democracy suspended.

> In view of the combinations of the lack of ideological appeal, low literacy rate, economic problems, communal and segmented social structure, and inflexibility of religious tradition, it is easy to be pessimistic about the future of democracy in the Middle East.[19]

Both traditional Islamic law and the dream of a united Islam weakened support for nation-state unity on its own terms which could evolve toward democracy. If kings and dictators are the primary unifying factors, in countries without strong middle classes, democratic evolution or revolution are unlikely. Other loyalties run toward clan, tribe, or family with a downplaying of individualism. The current administration's claims for the promotion of democracy as a cause for war in the Middle East seems naive. In light of a realistic sense of conditions for democracy such a war resulting in a resisted occupation might set back evolving forces encouraging democracy and lead to suppression of moderates or liberals who might support such forces. Still parliamentary government has supporters in Iran, Iraq, and Pakistan and the future remains open. Two of the largest democracies in the world, India and Indonesia, depend on Moslem support among other factors for survival. On a visit to meet the head of the Egyptian parliamentary committee on foreign policy, one could note that though the parliamentary building had been neglected it was now undergoing some belated repairs. Its long history of subservience under the Turks, British, and Egyptian rulers is not however very promising for democracy. It is only a little exaggeration to suggest that a military occupation of Iraq to promote democracy has roughly the same chance as a Saudi manipulation of its oil power to install a monarchy in the United States.[20]

The conflicts of Islamic and Christian nations, the violent domination of empires, and the violence of American democracy all encourage further inquiry into the human roots of violence.

Notes

1. Mahmoud M. Ayoub, *Islam Faith and History*, (Oxford: One World Publications, 2004), 228.

2. Reinhold Niebuhr, *The Structure of Nations and Empires*, (New York: Charles Scribner's Sons, 1959), 3.

3. *Ibid.*, 206.

4. Charles Norris Cochrane, *Christianity and Classical Culture: A Study of Thought and Action from Augustine to Augustus* (Oxford: Oxford University Press, 1940).

5. *Ibid.*, 442.

6. Reinhold Niebuhr, *Faith and Politics* (New York: George Braziller, Inc., 1968).

7. Cochrane, *Christianity and Classical Culture*, 501.

8. Reinhold Niebuhr, *The Nature and Destiny of Man* 2 vols. (New York: Charles Scribner's Sons, 1939).

9. Cochrane, *Christianity and Classical Culture*.

10. Reinhold Niebuhr, *The Structure of Nations and Empires* (New York Charles Scribner's Sons, 1959).

11. Charles Brown, ed. *A Reinhold Niebuhr Reader* (Philadelphia: Trinity Press International, 1992).

12. Cochrane, *Christianity and Classical Culture*, 515.

13. *Ibid.*, 448.

14. *Children of Light and Children of Darkness* (New York: Charles Scribner's Sons, 1944), 118.

15. *Ibid.*, xiii.

16. Reinhold Niebuhr and Paul Sigmund, *The Democratic Experience* (New York: Frederick A. Praeger, 1969), 55.

17. *Democratic Experience*, 123.

18. *Structure of Nations*, 123.

19. *Ibid.*, 116–18,121.

20. Pages 78–89 are scheduled for a forthcoming publication on Reinhold Niebuhr, edited by Daniel Rice, from Wm. B. Eerdmans.

CHAPTER SEVEN

Reflections on the Role of Violence

Hundreds of American citizens like myself have spent more time in the Middle East than the President of the United States or many of his advisors. We know a little about the complexity of relations among Moslems. We are not so quick to label whole countries as evil as the President or his advisors do. We know from our own failures both political and personal that we are sinners and that our knowledge is incomplete and biased. I have been received in Moslem homes, palaces, stores, shops, and Mosques from India, Kashmir, Turkey, Lebanon, Syria, Jordan, Egypt, and Palestine yet I understand so little that responsible participation requires study. I have also traveled extensively in Israel, visited synagogues in Russia during the Cold War, studied with and under Jewish teachers, counted Jews among my friends and political allies while also engaging in Christian-Jewish dialogues in the United States and Israel. Consequently here is a survey of helpful theories about religion and violence, and religion and terrorism, to assist Americans with religious interest to understand some of the complexities of the struggle. The theories studied after 9/11 are based on interviews with terrorists and others who had decades of experience with religion and politics of the Middle East. The government of Israel broke its appointments with our delegation to the Middle East because we spoke with Hezbollah at the time the church was considering divesting from selected companies that supported violence in the Middle East by business practices. Two years later Israel invaded the town we worshipped in and fought with our Hezbollah hosts. Would not diplomacy and dialogue and conversation have been better? Killing cannot be preferable.

During the 2006 Israel invasion of Lebanon news commentators repeatedly referred to Hezbollah as the enemy. Whose enemy?

Hezbollah's condemnation of al Qaeda's attacks on the United States was as strong as Arab nations formally allied with the United States. Fawaz A. Gerges quoted Arab experts indicating that Hezbollah and al Qaeda were more "foes than friends." The spiritual leader of Hezbollah gave dozens of sermons and lectures post 9/11 exposing al Qaeda's attack as illegitimate and not based on Islamic understanding regarding the non-violability of civilians. While Sayyed Mohammed Hussein Fadlallah opposed U.S. foreign policy he opposed killing American citizens who were innocent of decision making in foreign relations. Fadallah who became famous for supporting targeting of American forces in Lebanon denies the "clash of cultures" and denies that Islam supports attacks on civilians.

In his judgment targeting American civilians cannot be justified, but Israeli occupiers of Arab lands can be attacked. Israel he regards as a direct oppressor and a justified target. Shiite sources in Lebanon urged the American professor Gerges to pay more attention to Sunni Wahhabis who spawned bin Laden than to Shiites as the current terrorism was more the product of Sunni militants.[1]

If the most militant Shiites opposed, and Saddam Hussein opposed al Qaeda, more subtle forms of weapons to combat terrorism than M-1 tanks are obviously needed. The usual critique of Hezbollah condemns the organization for the attack upon the Marines in Beirut in 1983. I asked the Lebanese-American with our delegation about the charge. He said that Hezbollah was founded after that attack: several sources I've consulted have indicated Hezbollah was founded in 1982. The Shiites in Lebanon had been encouraged by Khomeni's success in establishing Islamic law in Iran. The Israeli invasion of 1982 encouraged the drift toward fundamentalist options and organizations. Amal founded by a friend of Khomeni in the 1970s became assertive with airplane hijackings and the attempts to establish Islamic government in Lebanon.[2] The civil war in Lebanon led to interventions by Israel, France, and the United States until the attacks on first the U.S. embassy and then the Marine barracks in 1983. Fifty-eight French soldiers were also killed by vehicle bomb explosions and the United States lost 251 military personnel.

Both Amal and Hezbollah have been accused of the attack on the American and French forces. An unknown group calling itself Islamic Jihad claimed credit for the attack. Vali Nasr wrote: "In October 1983, a suicide truck bomber almost certainly sent by Hezbollah killed 241 U.S. Marine peacekeepers at their lightly defended barracks in Beirut."[3] Further suicide attacks followed and European and American civilians were kidnapped, accompanied by demands that all French and Americans should depart Lebanon. The threat to the West in Lebanon was expressed in religious vocabulary, and it seemed to be a development of religious fanaticism. But interpreters like Fawaz A. Gerges do not believe religion was the cause of the resistance to the West.[4] He notes the surge in religious practice in the Muslim world in recent years and he finds religion carrying the protests against the social conditions of the Middle East. He rightly wants to avoid the demonization of Islam. The conflation of Islam and terrorism is certainly mistaken, but he seems to want to correct misinterpretation too far when he writes:

> Nonetheless, there is no direct correlation between religious fervor and militancy, despite what Western writers and journalists would like us to believe. Nor is there a direct correlation between religious fervor and political Islam despite what Islamists and jihadists would like us to believe.[5]

Despite all the references he makes to Islamists expressing their militancy in religious terms, he argues:

> Religion became their tool for political mobilization. Thus the key to understanding the jihadist and his journey lies in politics and not in religion.[6]

His book is a fascinating study of religious people acting politically and political protest being expressed in religious terms. He seems not to grasp that correlation in the discourse of religious studies is not causation but rather that there is a gap between A and B.[7] Neither A nor B cause each other, but certain expressions of A can reinforce and coexist with B. The bulk of Moslems can remain as he says "socially conservative" rejecting the murder of terrorism. But some interpretations of A can encourage B or are congruent with particular expressions of B.[8] When the correlations arise, then religion may, in some interpretations, under conditions of oppression, say as in Communist Eastern Europe or Islamic Middle East, become the legitimating rationale for resistance and revolution including violence. Other studies of violence and religion establish that most religions can contribute to the development of violence under various interpretations.

Gerges traced the development of an Egyptian Kamal who believed in violent tactics to overthrow an Egyptian government he regarded as secular and inappropriate. Violence failed, Kamal was jailed, and he came to repent of violent solutions. He spurned the arguments of Osama bin Laden as did most of Islam. Religious authorities did not protest American attempts to capture

Osama bin Laden in Afghanistan. The Islamic world acquiesced in American force to restore justice after 9/11 while much of the world applauded what promised to be a short, just war. But Kamal, like masses of other Moslems, read the invasion of Iraq differently. It was an unjust invasion of the community and resistance to occupation for many became a religious duty in terms of jihad. It seemed to be part of American hegemony and in particular oil imperialism. To Moslems it was easy to see the invasion of Iraq as part of the same American design to acquire oil from the central Asian republics of the former Soviet Union, and to build pipelines across Asia for its own power sources.

Orthodox Moslem approaches to violence would not support the outrages of 9/11, but they could much more easily support Moslem resistance to an American occupation of Iraq. Gerges presents the voice of Kamal al-Said Habib, an Egyptian theorist, for whom the invasion of Iraq ignited an inescapable conflict requiring jihad. Like many American commentators many Islamic voices could not support bin Laden's attack, but they are against the occupation of Iraq. Now the combinations of violence and religion are affected by the pragmatic needs of the Shiites versus the Sunnis. The ironic outcome of the United States and Israel's recent invasions of Shia homelands in Iraq and Lebanon has been to strengthen Shia dominance and inclinations toward theocracy in both countries. Hezbollah in Lebanon and Shia militia in Iraq are stronger than before the invasions, and both are allied to Iran.[9] Deeper investigations into theories of violence and religion complicate the issue to another degree.

Violence and Religion

The image of animals of prey snarling and fighting over a carcass on the African prairie evokes one explanation for the origins of violence in humanity. Today's story in the newspaper of two groups of Christian monks fighting with each other for control of a monastery on Mt. Athos suggests a different theory. My own interior reflection persuades me that I would resort to violence to protect myself or others. The first Biblical suggestion of violence in the story of Cain and Abel is over the proper way to express their spiritual nature through offerings given to God

Marjorie Suchocki's thesis on violence is that the human propensity to violence arises from our evolutionary history and that it becomes sin with the emergence of our human capacity for spirituality or transcendence. She puts it:

> My thesis is that the original sin is created through a triadic structure constituted by a propensity toward violence, by an interrelational solidarity of the

human species, and by social structures that shape the foundation of consciousness and conscience.[10]

Suchocki's thesis at this level is naturalistic. We survived as a species
killing for meat. This violence is built into us; we are one species and the social structures we have built reinforce the sin of unnecessary killing and so
we engage in it. The rest of the book affirms that sin is also rebellion against
God as well as rebellion against the misuse of creation, and that human anx-
iety so prominent in the twentieth-century existentialists is caused by violence. Traditional theology saw the original condition of human finitude
without trust in the divine, rebelling in pride and sloth against God to misuse creation. So what is original sin? Both existentialism and Suchocki agree
that sin is present before humans sin violently. Whether its origins are natural or spiritual it continues to shape humanity.

I assume, probably more than Suchocki does, that the modern theologies
she attacks, that is, those of Reinhold Niebuhr and Paul Tillich, have a relational evolutionary understanding of the world. They know that the development of human consciousness while setting us apart from earlier proto-hu-
man species reflects non-human origins. Neither evolution nor the
development of human consciousness is finished.

I think their explanation of sin depends less on archaeological-anthropo-
logical science than does Suchocki. For them neither meat eating nor private property explains sin out of which violence erupts. The world is not
nonviolent. From the sun's nuclear explosions to the animal food chain nature is violent. Western spirituality is primarily a story of human and not
natural spirituality. It presupposes humanity more than it scientifically explains humanity. Cain had his offering of the "fruit of the ground," and Abel
his sheep, and so there arose conflict in religious symbolic offerings. The
Biblical drama is about human violence and that is profoundly spiritual in
its origins.

But violence over mates, sexuality, and honor, for example, *The Iliad* and
The Odyssey, or over the land, *The Aenid*, are all deeply woven into the
foundations of human mythology. Our newspapers are filled daily with stories of violence over family issues, drugs, clothing, road rage, neuroses, and
so on. The human is broken and without adequate love and trust and with
social structures encouraging violence it erupts in a multitude of expressions. It is not necessary; most conflicts can be avoided. But our social structures encourage violence from the have-nots in protest and the violence by
the wealthy who manage the structures in denial of human expression that
it is *inevitable*.

It is very common to see peacemakers humiliate others in the peace movements of our time. Humiliation is in itself a form of aggression if not exactly violence. Even more human is our experience of countering violence with law and order and then finding that order to be violent. Life in the city reveals that those who possess the right to use deadly violence will often under pressure misuse it particularly against minorities. Biologically we have a capacity for violence, our human life is prone to violence, and without love, trust, and understanding we fall into it. Yet in such a world, the violent defense of self, others, aspects of civilization, or property may be necessary. Not all violence is sin. In a world of self-seeking and rebellion against God or more primarily in Suchocki's analysis "against creation" justified violence within defined limits is not sin, but a necessary response. Despite the grasping toward realism, Suchocki's conclusion, if I read it historically and not totally eschatologically, is a beautiful illusion. She wrote:

> We can be "recovering sinners," through. Through forgiveness we can receive, will, and act toward the well being of creation. By the grace of God, sin not withstanding, it is yet possible that all shall be well, and all shall be well, and all manners of things shall be well.[11]

Rene Girard's Theory

Rene Girard,[12] a Stanford literary critic, examined mythological and scriptural discussions or the origins of violence and its ritualization in religious structures. The evidence of his theory rests in detailed interpretations of literary classics, but his thesis can be explicated simply. The origin of violence rests in desire. This desire is encouraged by the attraction of someone else desiring an object or a person. One wants an object or experience because of the perception that someone else wants it. He calls the process "mimesis." It is mostly an unconscious process and it occurs after other basic needs have been met. Girard sees the Cain and Able story in this perspective. He could have turned to the book of James 4:2:

> You desire and do not have; so you kill, and you covet and cannot obtain; so you fight and wage war.

The desire turns to rivalry, then to violence through envy. The rivalry spirals into intensity and even more so in groups. Without countervailing power the desire leads groups into conflict.

Girard believes primitive groups could relieve the internal tensions of rivalry by sacrificing someone to the group's desire. The killing or expulsion of one from the group would relax the tension giving an illusion of peace. Gradually these sacrifices were built into regularly timed intervals to reinforce community peace. In modern society the dismissal of someone from employment or religious groups may relax tensions and create an illusion of peace. Children do it. Churches do it. Beleaguered administrations do it.

In Western religions the rituals of sacrifice are transmuted through history from human through animal to symbolic sacrifice. But what is still going on is ritual to reduce tension and restore peace. Girard seems to believe that the Bible fought against the sacrifice of humans (Abraham and Issac) and overthrew scapegoating in Jesus' sacrifice on the cross. The continuing life of the innocent sacrificed one reminded participants of the need for forgiveness to overcome the cycle of evil. If the believers in the reenactment of the crucifixion can focus their empathy on the victims of the society some of the oppression of that society can be decreased. The role of forgiveness emphasized as the nature of the divine encountered in the ritual has redemptive power for the society in a manner similar to the world transforming nature of forgiveness in Suchocki's argument.

My friend Robert Hammerton-Kelly has associated his work[13] with Girard's perspective. His writing and his collaboration with Girard at Stanford University's Center for International Security and Arms Control reflect his debt to Girard and to his own scholarship on Paul. He believes Paul's conversion on the road to Damascus reveals the truth about religion and therefore ultimately about politics. That truth is that our mimetic desire and its conflicts have been relieved through history by the sacrifice of people, animals, and symbols. The violence of our selves and our systems has been shielded from the exposure and transformation by this process of ritualistic scapegoating. Hammerton-Kelly presented his understanding of Girard's work with Girard present to the Presbyterian Church's task force on violence, religion, and terrorism. It impacted their work, but the task force composed of peace activists, ethicists, and political scientists did not absorb their analysis into the center of the report to the church. There were too many alternatives to consider. Or perhaps the task force was dominated by Christian realists who could not see historically that sacrifice and resurrection had overcome violence. Kristi Sparta, a psychologically informed graduate student, in her M.A. thesis on *Religion and Contemporary Terrorism*[14] reflected on Hammerton-Kelly, Rene Girard, and Gil Baille[15] and concluded: "Some would argue that it is not at all clear that resurrection stops violence." The sacrifice and resurrection event has in the majority of its representations been taken as a religious event with little consequence for the practical world of violent politics. The Girard thesis challenges that consensus fundamentally and Hammerton-Kelly suggests the church has misunderstood its founding message. "Our self-delusion in this religious world is monstrously mythical" as evidenced by our human failure to step aside and allow genocide to occur.[16]

Jurgensmeyer's Perspective

Mark Jurgensmeyer's *Terror in the Mind of God*[16] opens with an analysis of contemporary Christian terrorists. This is the appropriate beginning for a book on religious terrorism published in the United States. Despite its teachings of love, justice, and "turning the other cheek" Christianity has a bloody, violent history, and its violence has even been a means of religious conquest and conversions of populations. He begins with a study of Christian bombers of abortion clinics and explicates their theologies of violence. He then moves forward to the Christian Identity theologies of righteous violence and the bombing of the federal building in Oklahoma City. None of these bombings were approved of by the regular Christian churches, but in each case recognizable Christian arguments were woven together to make a case for self-justification by the bombers. All could appeal, they believed, to Christian justifications of violence. One bomber of women's clinics quoted Dietrich Bonhoeffer and Reinhold Niebuhr to argue his case. The bomber of the Oklahoma Federal Building who built his truck bomb according to plans found in William Pierce's *The Turner Diaries* reflected the theology of the Christian Identity movement. The Christian Identity movement is anti-Jewish and protheocratic government for the United States. Jurgensmeyer concludes his Christian terrorist chapter with discussion of the long-term Christian terrorists in Northern Ireland.

Juergensmeyer's award-winning book has the freshness of its research base in interviews he undertook. He once laughed with me about "The strange friends he has made in his interviews." The book shows the dark side of religion, but an aspect that the Girardians at least would regard as revealing deeper truths about religion. His descriptions based mostly on interviews but also grounded in the empirical research of others proceeds through Zionist violence, Islamic violence, focused on the World Trade Center early bombing, "Sikh and Hindu justifications for violence," and the Buddhist sectarian bombing in the Tokyo subways.

The second part of *Terror in the Mind of God*[18] seeks factors the acts of terror have in common. He finds the acts of terror to be "forms of public performance rather than aspects of political strategy." The idea of humanity involved in a cosmic war is a variable running through the stories of religious terrorists. They tend to regard the enemy they attack as demonic and think of themselves as religious martyrs. Through their attacks marginal people are empowered as they join the fight for the rule of God. Jurgensmeyer's interviews, stories, and analysis are so rich that it is impossible to summarize his work, but his summaries point toward the final work of this study which recommends action to counter religious terrorism. The difference in emphasis that I would place on the subject from Juregensmeyer is that I believe much religious terrorism is against the policies of the United States. Perhaps I see the issue this way both because of my emphasizing politics more and religion a little less than Jurgensmeyer. He summarizes the reasons why America has been the major target of terrorism in the late twentieth and early twenty-first centuries[19]:

1. America supports the enemies of the terrorists. America supported the Shah of Iran, the Saudis, and secular dictators in Islamic nations.
2. America has supported modern culture which in many ways violates traditional religious norms. Much of or religious terrorism is homophobic and terrorists often complain about toleration of homosexuality in the United States. Similarly males protecting their privileges find American feminism offensive.
3. American global economic reach is seen as offensive.
4. A fear of globalization encouraged by the United States is turned toward conspiracy theories buttressed by religious claims to make America appear as demonic.[20]

He summarizes the process by which the United States is perceived as a satanic power in a cosmic war as occurring through:

1. Real problems are perceived as expressive of a world gone wrong. Examples: Israel occupation of Palestine, corruption in U.S.-supported governments, modern society producing anomie and secularization, and decline of traditional taboos.
2. Terrorists tend to see regular political or social movements for change as closed to them or ineffective.
3. Religious symbols of Satan, cosmic war, extreme dualism are accepted and militant struggle moves toward violence providing religious, emotional hope of fighting for the divine.
4. Meaning is found in symbolic actions and in intense situations symbolic acts of violence may be chosen with religious justification.

One of the strengths of Jurgensmeyer's work is that as a theologically educated sociologist, he is able to interpret the religious ideas that inform particular terrorists who in the name of their ultimate concerns commit mass murder.

Jessica Stern introduces her book[22] with an examination of a Christian pastor who endorsed violence as a symptom of apocalyptic fulfillment. Kerry Noble, a Christian pastor, had his weaknesses played upon by Covenant of the Sword and the Arms of the Lord until he gave up personal perspectives and seemed to surrender his identity to the group. He came to believe in an immoral apocalypse and the need to be armed to participate. Anti-Jewish feelings were played upon to suspect the U.S. government and to plot its overthrow. He was eventually sentenced to five year's imprisonment for possession of unlicensed firearms. The leader of the cult was sentenced to twenty years imprisonment, but had his sentence reduced for testimony against others of his cult.

The leader, Ellison, had plotted to blow up the Murrah Building in Oklahoma City. His associate, Richard Snell, was sentenced to die for two murders on April 19, 1995. Snell's prophecy of an explosion on his death was fulfilled when Timothy McVeigh who had been phoning Ellison's compound blew up the Alfred P. Murrah Federal Building in Oklahoma City.[23] Stern entitled the chapter on pastor Noble "Alienation." Proceeding further in her study she discussed other sources: many particular Moslems find the new world "humiliating." The threatened traditions produce "emergency conditions." But, she also found motivations of "greed for political power, wounded masculinity and the use of these for 'Holy Wars' masking atrocities."[24]

Kristi Sparta[25] found Stern's work especially helpful in explaining the development of women terrorists. The late Yassir Arafat was particularly instrumental in bringing women into the role of martyrdom. His secular coalition was earlier than the more religious Hamas in enlisting women for sacrifice. Threatened maleness has had a lot to do with encouraging terrorism. But here Arafat finding resistance to martyrdom in his movement spoke on behalf of women's martyrdom. The cases that Jessica Stern investigated revealed women volunteering who had no future of significance in Palestinian society or who had been humiliated or who had been raped or who were infertile. In one case a father fearing that the success of his family in devastated Palestine was resulting in threats to his family encouraged his humiliated daughter to seek martyrdom and earn his family respect. Following Arafat's success in recruiting female suicide bombers, Hamas also shifted its policy and recruited women for suicide and murder called religious martyrdom. The women were even promised equality at Allah's table in Heaven. The most detailed examination[26] of women Moslem bombers uses Arafat's title for them: "Army of Roses." I had hoped to engage him in dialogue about this issue, but the interview was cancelled when we were on our way to his compound because of his last and fatal illness.

Terrorism diverse in its origins continues to evolve. Bin Laden provides inspiration even when he cannot direct, and lone wolf operators and indigenous cells spring up and attack in various countries. The war in Iraq increases terrorist attacks upon civilians and resistance attacks against the U.S. occupiers. The civil, religious war between Sunnis and Shias has its own history in the Middle East which is only complicated by a thin veneer of control by the U.S. occupiers. Even the gains in Afghanistan have been largely wasted as the Taliban returns to engage in both terrorism and armed resistance. The religious language intensifies the conflicts and for some participants the religious wars become absolute while for others the same wars serve greed. This is not all that different from the occupying U.S. perspective as various motives of patriotism, religion, or democratization are accompanied by motivations of pride, and more important, greed. Of special significance for the future is the evolution of Shia power in Iraq. In writing on terrorism by the Shia in the 1980s, I emphasized their campaign to remove the U.S. influence from the region. That is still a goal and the U.S. alliance with Shia power in Iraq is only a temporary, useful alliance from a Shia perspective regardless of the illusions of the United States about new secular democratic forms of government that the United States may promote.

Notes

1. Fawaz A. Gerges, *Journey of the Jihadist: Inside Muslim Militancy* (New York: Harcourt, Inc., 2006), 189.

2. *Ibid.*, 191.

3. Vali Nasr, *The Shia Revival* (W. W. Norton & Company, 2007) 143.

4. Gerges, *Journey of the Jihadist*, 87.

5. *Ibid.*, 90.

6. *Ibid.*, 11.

7. Paul Tillich, *Systematic Theology*, I (Chicago: University of Chicago Press, 1951).

8. Tillich's use of the term *correlation* has some congruence with Max Weber's use of psychological affinity in *The Protestant Ethic and the Spirit of Capitalism* (New York; Charles Scribner's Sons, 1958).

9. Vali Nasr, "When the Shiites Rise," *Foreign Affairs* (July/August, 2006), 58–74.

10. Marjorie Suchocki, *The Fall to Violence* (New York: Continuum,1994).

11. *Ibid.*, 165. Partially quoted from Julian of Norwich.

12. Rene Girard, *Violence and the Sacred* (Baltimore: John Hopkins University Press, 1977).

13. Robert Hammerton-Kelly, "Violence and Religion," *Church and Society* (May/June, 3004), 35–44.

14. Kristi Sparta, *Religion and Contemporary Terrorism* (Unpublished Master of Arts Thesis, Pittsburgh Theological Seminary, 2004), 16.

15. Gil Baille, *Violence Unveiled* (New York: Crossroad Publishing, 1995).

16. Hammerton-Kelly, 43.

17. Mark Juergensmeyer, *Terror in the Mind of God: The Global Rise of Religious Violence* (Berkley: University of California Press, 2003). Professor Jurgensmeyer was a student colleague of mine at Union Theological Seminary and in the International Fellows Program of Columbia University in the 1960s.

18. *Ibid.*, xi.

19. *Ibid.*, 184–85.

20. See: Ismael Garcia, "Reflections on Imperialism, Violence and Terrorism," *Church and Society* (May/June, 2004), 45–65.

21. *Ibid.*, 188–89.

22. Jessica Stern, *Terror in the Name of God: Why Religious Militants Kill* (New York: Harper/Collins Publisher, 2003).

23. *Ibid.*, 29.

24. *Ibid.*, xix.

25. Sparta, 35–45.

26. Barbara Victor, *Army of Roses: Inside the World of Palestinian Women Suicide Bombers* (New York: Rodale, Inc., 2003) as quoted by Sparta, 36.

CHAPTER EIGHT

~

Response to Terrorism and the War in Iraq

The preceding chapters have argued that it is necessary to understand religion and to think realistically about conflict and peacemaking to comprehend the present struggles in the Middle East. Classical realist thinkers understood as morally concerned persons like Herbert Butterfield, Reinhold Niebuhr, George Kennan, Hans J. Morgenthau, Paul Tillich, and John C. Bennett all had strong religious convictions and they all served their religious communities. They might have all been surprised by the outbreak of so much religiously based violence in the twenty-first century. Madeleine Albright admits to being surprised and she calls for training of diplomats in religious studies.[1] I following Reinhold Niebuhr have been calling for theological students to be trained in internationals relations since the 1960s.[2] To date neither of us had many followers on these issues. The general inattention to religious studies of other cultures by American education left the United States relatively ignorant in face of religiously inspired attacks. Even more dangerous was the lacunae in the study of Islam which left the United States naive as to the consequences within Islam of our support for Israel's policies. So sobered by religious violence our search for a model of response to terrorism and the invasion of Iraq leads to a realist stance informed by religious studies. Abraham and the prophets are the heritage of all three faiths in the conflict, and they may show guidelines to the way out of our trauma when expressed in prudent realist terms. The strengths of prophetic religion rest in its articulation not in holy war conquest or occupied apocalyptic, but at a time of political responsibility, Amos, Jeremiah, Isaiah, Elijah, and Elisha were all expert in international affairs, and they all demanded justice. Isaiah's perspective on reality and his vision of a possible peace was expressed again by Jeremiah and Micah.[3]

Edward Long, Jr.'s fine book[4] on responding to terrorism suggests for us three models of response: international law and just peacemaking. He suggests the choice of model might be more fundamental than detailed recommendations because of the novelty of terrorist actions in different situations. He clearly preferrs the response that utilizes international law and treats terrorists as criminals. He observed the developments of crusade response and regards the U.S. response since 9/11 as reflecting a Crusade pattern though not necessarily religious. I've differed with Professor Long in this description believing that "Crusade" requires authoritative religious sanction and these had been withheld from the wars with Iraq. There is no papal sanction for the U.S. war; rather the Vatican has tried to restrain the war. Major denominations in the United States have urged the restraint from war and criticized the present wars against Iraq. Fundamentalist preachers and conservative religious groups along with others have supported the wars and both Presidents Bush have claimed religious authority for their wars. But claiming a war is just or that it is God's will neither makes it so nor raises it to a level of a crusade though it may be thought of as a crusade by some. I believe the Shia-Sunni conflicts and the Jewish-Moslem conflicts are better described as religious wars rather than crusades. The U.S. response has elements of religious response in it and those running U.S. foreign policy would not be directing the war except for fundamentalist and evangelical votes in 2000 and 2004.

Just war categories are rather abstract and while they provide a classical rationale for debates about a war, they do not resolve any issues in themselves. Alan Geyer and Barbara Green convincingly argued against President G.H.W. Bush's justification of the first Iraq war in just war terms.[5] The first Iraq war as well as the second failed the tests of rigorous just war analysis. Ethical analysis can resort to just war criteria without regarding them as the most adequate way to think about war.

Three contemporary religious ethics books on these wars have all used just war categories while noting the traditions of crusade or holy war, and pacifism. All have pointed to resources in the three religious traditions of justice seeking and just peacemaking. Long developed this new possibility along with Green and Geyer while Kenneth Vaux attached more relevance to holy war thinking.[6] The classical political realists mentioned above did not put so much weight on crusade or just war categories. This realism is less optimistic than the just peacemaking model, but in my opinion no less concerned about the pursuit of peace. Their writing is more focused on diplomacy than just peacemaking and more inclined to make judgments from political theory and to ground their reflections historically. Elsewhere[7] I have argued that some of the realists were Zionists and that they did not account adequately for Moslem resistance to Israel. Their sense of prudent, national self-limitation freed them from the temptations of the neoconservative imperialism. But in their concern to protect Jews who had suffered the calamity of the Nazi Holocaust, they neglected to understand how colonial an imposition the occupation of Arab lands by first European Jews and then the Jews of the diaspora would seem to the Moslem world.

The United Nations Charter reflects a model of concern for peace that is realistic. Article 33 of Chapter VI requires, in conflict situations: negotiations, enquiry, mediation, conciliation, arbitration, judicial settlement, and regional solutions of other peaceful means. The attempt by the United Nations to divide Israel and Palestine into two separate states with an international Jerusalem has not worked. Israel military success has allowed it to occupy in defiance of U.N. resolutions the original Palestine of which it was to receive approximately 55 percent originally.

In its attempt to influence and to dominate the Middle East, the United States at different times allied with two radically different Mideast leaders: Saddam Hussein and Osama bin Laden. In the long run neither proved to be reliable allies. Both of these allies presented the United States with extreme difficulties and the United States government has at times neglected the hostility of the one for the other and warred against both of them. The war against the attacker of the United States, Osama bin Laden, was widely supported by the United Nations and most nations of the world. The first Gulf War to liberate Kuwait was more controversial, but it had United Nations sanction and considerable international support. The second Gulf War has not been rationally justified nor supported by most of the nations of the world. However given the U.S. appetite for oil and the desire on the part of some to have military bases in Iraq or even to pursue the illusory goal of creating a client democratic state in Iraq it is not surprising to find the United States involved in wars in the region to arrange the delivery of oil resources on terms favorable to American corporate interests.

The term of *prophetic realism* is used to describe a model of response, though others use the terms *ethical realism* or *moral realism*. Prophetic realism utilizes in-depth historical perspectives like those used by Geyer and Green and is open to, but not dependent on, just war categories. Its concerns are for national self-limitation by a powerful United States, a capacity to criticize both U.S. policy and Israeli policy, or the policies of other countries as Amos criticized the violations of the surrounding countries. The other prophets were intentionally concerned to apply standards of justice to their own country's policy. There is also a determination to speak in moral terms, but in terms of discourse that are relevant to the language of the elite who formulate foreign policy. Because many of its sources are from religious sources it is open to including the resources from religious studies, and this is particularly so in the cases of religious terrorism and religious wars. After four years of war, U.S. foreign policy language has finally recognized that much of the war in Iraq is a civil war. Of course, in truth there is very little that is civil about it, and it is obviously, in large part, a religious war within Islam while the U.S. war is driven by fundamentalist support for the presidency of George Bush, and support for the policies of Israel which is also in part religious support from some Christians and Jews. Another reason for recommending prophetic realism as a model of response is that the just war categories run afoul of two realities. First as Kenneth Vaux[8] suggested just war theory does not make clear, itself, how many criteria of the just war (see chapter 2) have to be met for a war to be regarded as just. Second, though the conditions for engaging in a necessary war might be met, the actual processes (i.e., means) of a war are seldom just. A war on balance might be justifiable, but the carrying out of wars always runs afoul of the restrictions to refrain from torture, avoid lying, protect civilians, proportional use of force, and so on. The actual goals of wars to establish peace are only rarely met. Violence leads to resentment, anger, and reaction toward more violence. The first Gulf War leads to the second Gulf war and then to the religious wars between Shia and Sunni. The liberation of Afghanistan from the Russians leads to the domination of the country by the Taliban and to al Qaeda's attacks upon the United States, and to the U.S. occupation of Afghanistan. Augustine as the early articulator of his mentor Ambrose's insights about just war was correct when he said a Christian could only enter a war sorrowfully. This moral perspective or realism does not want to say a war is just as much as it regretfully argues some wars are justifiable while most are not.

The three excellent ethics books on war in the Gulf that I've mentioned here all concluded with different versions of just peacemaking policies and not with affirmations of prophetic or moral realism. Geyer and Green and Long all had several reservations about realism. The perspective informing the following recommendations shares the concerns of just peacemaking but is less optimistic about international structures emerging to limit the nations. It tends to see international politics as a competitive system with rules which are often set aside. It appreciates efforts of citizen groups and nonviolent promotion of peace and justice organizations while still emphasizing the role of elites in foreign policy who are only episodically deferential to citizens' pressures. In the United States' elections can to some extent change the elites. In Iran elections and parliamentary actions have more weight than they did in Iraq. In some Arab countries like Kuwait and Saudi Arabia feudal family rule is the norm; in others like Egypt a dictator is more responsive to civil society. While some of the following recommendations are congruent with just peacemaking recommendations by churches, the just peacemaking project, and the writings of Ed Long, Jr., Barbara Green, and Alan Geyer, some of them assume that the blockages to peace are more intractable than those the authors have specified.

Recommendations

The perspective affirmed here of a prophetic realism acknowledges that when there is a dispute both sides must make the adjustments to reach a settlement based on compromise and balances of power. The argument of the whole book is that the United States is confronting a religious war founded upon religiously laden disputes. The United States can make adjustments and must; it can affect some alterations in the responses of its religious opponents, but it cannot in itself end jihad. Only Moslems can interpret jihad in ways that dries up support for religious war against the United States. Jihad cannot be defeated by U.S. occupation of Moslem countries for occupation produces the jihadists. The United States can hope that the balance of opposition to U.S. policy has not tipped so against the United States that it cannot be reversed. Did our response to 9/11 like the Emperors of Germany and Russia's response to the assassination of Archduke Ferdinand tip us into a war from which there is no exit until like Russia and Germany both empires are destroyed? I think not; an exit is still possible if the United States can move with boldness, even if that boldness must wait upon a new U.S. administration. A former supporter of the war, Thomas L. Friedman, now sees that any solution to the war will require "Islam finds a way for its sects to get along."[9] Wiser U.S. leadership would have understood from the beginning that breaking the Baathist regime would fuel the Shia revival stemming from Iran, and that the Sunnis would not accept militant Shia dominance. So hoping that wise U.S. policy initiatives and changes in U.S. policy and unknown but hoped-for changes from within Islam can turn away from the religious warfare aspects of jihad to its peaceful and justice-seeking components, we move to recommending policy.

1

Realism insists we must defend ourselves appropriately. Competitive sports require both good defense and good offense, staying within the rules of the game, and appropriate equipment. During the shift from the Clinton administration to the second Bush administration valuable defensive planning against terrorism received a very low priority for months as emphasis was place upon war planning more appropriate for the Cold War. Key figures in the new administration, particularly Donald Rumsfeld and Richard Cheney, were cold warriors from the previous Bush administration and their eyes were on missiles, new doctrines of *blitzkrieg* warfare with fewer troops, high-technological weapons, and world domination. Most of these issues were irrelevant to the war in which we found ourselves.[10] Richard A. Clarke[11] made the indictment regarding the neglected counterterrorism policies. Soviet experts like Condoleeza Rice were not well suited for dealing with Middle Eastern problems and Powell's previous experience with the Middle East was squandered as he resisted invading and then surrendered his judgment to stronger colleagues and obviously mistaken intelligence reports. The President was beyond the depth of his experience and like the prodigal son he squandered his inheritance in distant lands.

The United States might have succeeded in Afghanistan in capturing or killing the leadership of al Qaeda, but before the job was finished the energy and imagination supplied early by the C.I.A. was not reinforced by the needed U.S. forces to finish the job as attention was diverted to Iraq. Rumsfeld's folly of limited forces trumped the Powell doctrine of massive force to accomplish the goal and goals were not achieved. The hunting of al Qaeda after 9/11 was obviously morally justified as a defensive action against an organization that had repeatedly struck the installations and the homeland of the United States. It was Pearl Harbor all over again and the intervention in Afghanistan had a just cause. The attack on Iraq, however, would make an analogy only if Franklin D. Roosevelt had attacked Argentina after Pearl Harbor. The Defense Department's focus on Iraq doomed the intervention in Afghanistan to fail in its goal and to the continuation of the Taliban's jihad or religious war against the United States. Jihads often fail. At this time maybe the government in Kabul can succeed, but in any case the pursuit of al Qaeda's original leaders must be energized and carried through to a successful conclusion. Al Qaeda's attacks on the United States were not supported by much of the Moslem world, and the proper mix of covert and overt force may still produce success. The greatest danger from bin Laden is not his capacity to hurt the United States, but his ability to provoke the United States into overreaction and dangerous policies. Measures by Homeland Security and other U.S. forces need to be adjusted through experience as the struggle continues.

The defense of the United States is both a unilateral and a multilateral operation and many countries are contributing to the apprehension of al Qaeda and the thwarting of terrorist plans. Some allies like Saudi Arabia and Pakistan have been less energetic than the United States had a right to expect. Other allies would have rightly restrained the United States from invading Iraq, but, alas, the administration would not wait in its hasty planning to seize and remake the desperate nation of Iraq. The planning for the war left out the need to provide adequate forces to occupy the country.

The short term of Paul L. Bremer as director of the Coalition Provisional Authority was characterized by confusion in the chain of command,[12] and dismissal of the Iraq Army and the leadership of the governmental agencies produced chaos. The struggle between the State Department and the Defense Department began in 2001 and did not moderate until Secretary of State Rice succeeded in ousting Donald Rumsfeld in 2007. Her recommendation of Robert Gates to replace the failed Donald Rumsfeld restored some harmony in the leadership of the occupation, but by then many opportunities had been wasted. The fate of the United States in Iraq hangs on how indigenous religious leadership chooses to act. There will be neither peace nor order without religious peace and that involves the balance of power between Sunni and Shia.

Senator Webb's response to the 2007 "State of the Union" address made it clear that in his perspective the task is to fight anti–United States terrorists and not to engage in risky international wars. Multinational help and cooperation is essential to fight and apprehend international terrorist threats to U.S. people and interests.

Many have regarded the candlelight opposition to the invasion of Iraq as the largest anti-war demonstration in the history of the world. The majority of the protesters were not demonstrating against hunting criminals who command terrorist acts. They were protesting against an invasion which the President's father and most of his advisors regarded as unwise. Even in 1991 when Iraq's invasion of U.S. ally Kuwait provided a rationale for the first Gulf War, Alan Geyer and Barbara Green's *Line in the Sand*[13] provided a quite complete just war analysis against that war. To summarize: The first recommendation is that the defense of the United States be conducted in a prudent manner, that the just war limitations on war be affirmed, and that the priority of peace and sadness of war be recognized by the United States as it was in the original spokesmen for just war, Augustine and Thomas Aquinas.

2

The U.S. commitment to international law and organizations was expressed in the founding of the United Nations. As World War II required an alliance, preservation of the peace required diplomacy and organization. The ideological, economic struggle between the United States and the U.S.S.R. thwarted the world's hopes for international law and organization. The end of the Cold War gave birth to new hopes for law and order. Both the ideological and religious debts of the Bush administration prevented the grasping of the opportunity in a rush toward a more assertive, unilateral policy. Neoconservative thinkers wanted more assertive, unilateral policy initiatives. Fundamentalist religious leaders were suspicious of international law and order which could limit the United States. On the other hand the just peacemaking critics of the Bush administration (see chapter 3) were hopeful for United Nations' strengthening. Mainline and Catholic religious consensus pushed in terms reminiscent of Isaiah's vision of ordered peace for more law and order, but this influence was negligible in the White House counsels.

Another administration returning to the American emphasis on law and order will process and then reform, if necessary, treaties against nuclear weapons testing, anti-ballistic missile defense, the Kyoto environmental treaty, and particularly for defense against terrorism the International Criminal Court. Unratified Human Rights Conventions need to be pushed forward as well as all the opinions rendered against the Geneva War accords by this recent administration need to be rendered null.

The United States' voice on human rights has been silenced for the years of the Iraq war. It could not have been heard well as the charges of U.S. torture and unilateral emphases would have drowned out human rights language. Another administration as it disengages from Iraq will have an opportunity to return to human rights as the moral dimension of international relations language. Of course, human rights language has its political dimensions, but its establishment as moral language heightens the importance of its role.[12] Reforms or elimination of both the Patriot Act and the Guantanamo Bay prison will match with actions the needed shift in rhetoric.

3

An American shift from militarism to diplomacy would decrease terrorist attacks upon the country. There is a high correlation between terrorism and foreign military occupation of a country. All of the recent religious terrorism against Americans by foreign forces is attributable to opposition against U.S. military presence in Lebanon, Saudi Arabia, Iraq, and support for Israel's occupation of Palestine in the last three decades.

Americans are overly tempted to solve problems with technology and military force. Donald Rumsfeld's Department of Defense budgets and military response to Iraq are examples of this tendency. Other countries live more peaceably in the world than the United States. Since the end of the Cold War, the U.S.'s first was neglectful of important international realities and then in the last eight years has tried to dominate the world. United States' diplomats and business people can operate in the region of the Middle East without U.S. military control. It is not a major concern of the United States whether the ancient cultures and newer nation-states of that huge populous region are governed by one form of government or another. Islam under the pressures of poverty and globalization will have many internal struggles, but we have neither the power nor the understanding to rule that world. While there is no need for the United States to rule either Europe or Japan, vital partnerships with these powers are essential to the security of the United States. Listening to European reluctance to reengage in dominating Asia would be a wise move for the United States. Islam's divisions are their ancient fights and not particularly our business. High-technological U.S. interference will make most of these worse and less subject to compromise settlements. The internecine warfare with its ancient religious meanings in the divisions between the Shiites and Sunnis excuses the United States from the need to continue to try and resolve that country's problems. The U.S. government has not yet recognized the religious nature of the war or at least it has not named it as a religious war, as it surely is. The origins of the power struggles ruining Iraq are way beyond the capacity of the United States to resolve. The United States should not have invaded Iraq as it had reduced it to impotence under air control and sanctions, and U.N. inspections were working. But Iraqi murders of each other are not morally justified either. Under occupation the United States had responsibilities to maintain law and order, but Iraqis did not lose any of their responsibilities to refrain from terrorism, murder, and destruction. If sufficient numbers of Iraqis want a religious civil war, then it is their fate to endure it for a season until they sort out their new compromises. It is not the responsibility of the United States to continue to take sides in an ancient religious struggle that predates the United States by 1,000 years. As a former occupying power and a customer for Iraq's oil, the United States will have a continuing role to play diplomatically, but the sooner the military occupation ends, the sooner the Iraqis will determine their own future and quell the killing.

The just peacemaking arguments to reduce war by reducing the worldwide distribution of armaments have been echoed in previous writing[14] so I will not belabor them here. Several features of increasing the armament in the world contribute to making the United States less secure. The United States is the major arms merchant to the world, and particularly to the poorer nations of the world. Subsidized arms transfers, promotion of sale of U.S. armaments, small arms shipments, militarization of space, new nuclear weapons developments, and support for the military machines of Israel and Egypt all make the United States less secure. A U.S. military expenditure of more than the next six nations combined can be halved with no loss of security to the United States. American idealism and self-interest both threaten peace and a less fully armed America will be less tempted to military adventurism than an overly armed United States. The arms reduction programs of the United States should be coupled with serious negotiations for other countries to reduce their arms development as well. Less support to military forces in the Islamic world will reduce the U.S. compulsion to intervene militarily. The financial savings will also make it more possible to pursue justice for the uneducated and medically underserved Americans.

Part of the movement away from militarism toward diplomacy is for the United States to value peace more highly. Realists recognize that part of international relations is the competition and clash of differing foreign policy interests of semi-autonomous actors. But the morally concerned of them always recognized that the struggle was foremost a struggle to maintain peace. Niebuhr talked repeatedly of the partnership between competitive U.S.S.R. and United States in protecting the peace. Morgenthau's subtitle of his classic of political realism *Politics among Nations* was *The Struggle for Power and Peace*, and so was the content of the volume. The insertions of U.S. military force into the region—Reagan in Lebanon, Bush in Iraq, and Bush again in Iraq—forgot this goal of policy. More sensitivity to the history of Islam and its capacity to turn its religious teaching of jihad into ongoing holy war could have reinforced a commitment to prudentially refrain from military reliance on intervention and occupation. Of course, the diplomacy of some countries is reinforced by military capacity, economic power, and ideological or moral leadership. However the most powerful countries are always in danger of alliances forming against their power. The United States has historically led such alliances vis-à-vis European *realpolitik*. Decreasing the militarization of U.S. foreign policy removes some of the irritants that lead to organized religious terrorist acts and increases U.S. security. The proposals in the candidate presidential position papers of Mitt Romney and Barack Obama to increase the U. S. armed forces are moves in the wrong direction.[15]

4

Important in its own terms, but also useful for reducing support for terrorist attacks, would be U.S. leadership of a serious effort to reduce world poverty and move toward sustainable human development in the poor nations of the world. U.S. international aid to fight poverty has declined and confidence in it has fallen. The Bush administration's turn to fund aspects of Africa's struggle with AIDS has been an important commitment. Evangelical support for Africa and lobbying for Africa has been a valuable contribution from that religious revival. My own local, liberal church has also made generous gifts toward fighting AIDS in Africa and micro-lending development projects, particularly OIKO credit. But as generous as foundations, church, and private aid for development of poor people has been, the U.S. government will have to join with other nations to relieve the suffering. Walking with my Peace Corps daughter in West Africa has shown me villages with almost no possessions and just enough food to avoid starvation. Other parts of Africa are less fortunate. Slavery and squalor run through much of the Southern hemisphere. A new administration could regain moral credibility for the United States in leadership to overcome poverty where in many cases it is starvation unto death.

Strong forces abroad resist economic development of the masses. Governments, robber barons, and feudal lords profit from the way things are and they must be changed if the people are empowered. Tax structures, tariffs, corruption, governance all conspire to keep 2 billion of the world's people very poor and hundreds of thousands enslaved. So a world wide campaign against this poverty will encounter wide spread resistance as did the eighteenth- and nineteenth-century campaign to reduce slavery. It may never have complete success, but the commitment to seriously engage poverty would provide a material base to support recognition of American moral ideals.

5

Peace in the Middle East requires both the security of Israel and the termination of its expansion since the 1967 war. Majority Israeli and Arab support recognizes the gains of 1967 and will accept them as a border as long as Jerusalem is a shared city and Palestine can have a capital there. A compromise will recognize the unique nature of the two or three states and promote the concept of all of Islam, Judaism, and Christianity as heirs of Abraham. It is clear that responsible Arab leadership backed by the United States can accept and live with such a settlement, and so would most of Israel. As the United States used economic pressure to delegitimize Hamas and to encourage Israel's settlement policies, so it must move toward delegitimizing the illegal settlements by a reduction of military aid to Israel. A reduction of one billion per year until the settlements are turned over to Palestinian authority would seem a reasonable inducement to end the greatest barrier to peace while increasing Israel's security. Similarly renewed payments to Palestine cannot be Condoleezza Rice's commitment to give the Palestinian Authority whatever it asks.[16] Aid must be accompanied by progress politically and on the ground to end terrorism against Israel.

6

Dialogue toward understanding requires a recognition that without peace among religions there is no peace. The interreligious dialogue among all the Jewish divisions, the Moslem parties, and the Christian sects must proceed apace and with more attention to the political expression of religion. The rules in all the societies against murder and the religious limitations on war need to be taught and discussed among the traditions. There are meager expressions of this dialogue in important Arab cities and within Israel. However, the lack of interest by the U.S. government in such dialogue reveals the naivete of U.S. policy makers and the longstanding neglect of religious studies within international relations studies. Great Britain did not understand Hinduism or Gandhi until they had lost India. The United States follows along in its secular innocence but consequently misunderstands the religious wars of the Middle East. Most of the world integrates its religious commitments more fully into state policy than the United States. While supporting various "The wall of separation of Church and State," for the United States it is not the way of most of the world. The costs and risks of serious interreligious dialogue are great, but the resultant wisdom would decrease the U.S. attacks upon the Middle East.

7

It is improbable that any other administration of the United States than one dominated by oilmen would have invaded Iraq. The defense of oil interests was more obvious in the first Gulf War than the second. Hussein had demanded reunion with Kuwait to prevent slant drilling across the border, clear access to an oil port, and compensation for his war against Iran. The threat of one state combining Iraq and Kuwait's resources and threatening the oil fields of Arabia was too much. It was a long-held policy that Gulf oil resources were a vital U.S. interest. In the second Gulf War the oil interests were clouded under issues of terrorism, weapons of mass destruction, and democracy, all of which were, in the case of Iraq, illusions. Yet it was assumed oil would pay for the rebuilding of Iraq and a vital issue for the Shiite government in U.S. perspective was the denationalizing of the oil resources to open them to multinational corporate control. So oil as an issue was somewhat hidden, but it has been the dominant issue for Western influence since Great Britain, France, and the United States divided up the oil resources of the dismembered Ottoman Empire after World War I. The Council on Foreign Relations has estimated the reserves in Iraq at 220 billion barrels of oil or one quarter of the world's known potential resources. Even if not proven, the oil resources worth maybe 30 trillion dollars are sufficient motivation for a neo-conservative, oil-informed administration to seek.[17]

Ecological threats are combining with the cost of oil, global warming, and Middle Eastern politics to finally incline the United States toward a combination of conservation and alternative energy sources to reduce U.S. dependence on the Middle East.

The Bush administration, partially dominated by Haliburton's vice-president, Richard Cheney, has been slow to move on alternative energy sources or conservation, but most of the serious candidates to replace them see the need for deep changes in energy policy.

The enormous energy consumption of war and of maintaining unnecessary naval fleets in the Mediterranean Sea, Persian Gulf, and Indian Ocean also increase the dependence of the United States on the very countries which supply the energy. Many of these countries especially Saudi Arabia, present real dangers to the United States as long as the United States attempts to dominate them. Distant unnecessary wars have ruined many empires and U.S. prudence in the face of the neoconservative and nationalist pressure to dominate other countries is needed.

8

Globalization is a driving force in most societies. Like capitalism or socialism it must be evaluated by standards of justice and moderated to protect the environment and to protect human welfare. It holds promise for the movement of some of the world's poor into the world economy. This is more true for India and China than for many of the poor countries of Africa. Issues of declining human welfare are engendering resistance to globalization in Latin America. Religiously led militants are resisting American domination under the flag of globalization. In the long run it is doubtful that Europe will sacrifice much of its own welfare or interests for an American-led globalization. Certain leadership sectors of the financial, manufacturing, and trading world clearly profit from globalization, but many others do not. American inequality of income and wealth develop under the mobility of capital in the global-

ization process.[18] The stalling of the Doha round of agricultural tariffs and reduction of agricultural subsidies has been mostly at the expense of the less
powerful nations and groups of the world. The protection of health-related
property rights to Western powers especially the United States contributes to
suffering in the poorer part of the world. The destruction of the U.S. middle
class' economic prosperity built in the manufacturing industry does not bode
well for American democracy or welfare. Prophetic realism is as concerned
about justice at home as well as peace abroad. Major issues at home include
just living wage, improved education, universal health care, progressive tax-
ation, immigration reform, and civil rights. Corporations need to be made to
be subservient to the public and to answer to human values exercised
through international and national institutions. Whether particular expressions promote real cooperation or domination is a guide to the need for promotion or resistance to these powerful factors.

In its founding the United Nations was committed to decolonization and
the movement of peoples for independence hurriedly dismantled the British
and French empires. Paris and London had developed a form of globalization
continuing the European imperialism of the sixteenth century to the twentieth century. That imperialism has been both corporate and national. The
spirit to free peoples from domination of central powers is real and can become a more powerful force than it now appears to be. The world is too diverse to be subject to one power or style of organization and unity under one
or two central powers should not be expected.

9

On the morality of United States policy, the best way forward is the responsive model of H. Richard Niebuhr carried forward in a progressive spirit promoting values of equality, freedom and order under law with the pragmatism
of William James, John Dewey, and Reinhold Niebuhr. American foreign
policy leadership must be drawn from sectors of the country that know very
well what is going on in the world. Wide reading, travel, and governmental
experience are necessary prerequisites of a truly responsive foreign policy reflecting American values. The American ideals of equality, liberty, and order
under law are often betrayed by America, but they are real values to be pursued. The world arena reveals the relativity of moral standards to history and
culture as Ernst Troeltsch taught at the beginning of the war-filled twentieth
century. So the United States is not served well by crusades or overemphasis
of American goals. Six percent of the world population deserves to contribute to the world dialogue to the extent of its creativity relative to the others. World politics has both structures and institutions for cooperation and

anarchic features. Careful listening and intense dialogue based on great learning is the best way forward in a world in which our morality must respond to the moral perceptions of others. Pragmatic realism cannot become an excuse for domination, imperialism, and war but should serve to provide counsels of prudence and reminders of the fate of nations that have overreached their resources.

Religious communities will contribute to these debates with their own unique perspectives. The more they can express their values in the general public discourse of American political morality, the more guidance they can provide for officials who have to act for the whole country and not in terms of particular sectarian convictions.

10

Finally, the book has articulated many standards of behavior for foreign policy. The chapter on just peacemaking affirmed the action practices of that perspective. The chapter on just war affirmed the principles of just war as realistic guidelines for international conduct. I regard all of these counsels as wise and if combined with an ultimate commitment, as much as it is in us, to live peaceably with all, the United States would avoid needless wars and the destruction of the poor, the women, and the children which make up most of the casualties of modern warfare. The action practices of peacemaking and the rigorous criteria for justifying any war are received in a context of listening to what is moving in the world. Listening promotes the necessary dialogues and elevates the practice of wise diplomacy to keep us in our strength from pride and over reaction to protests against our power. Our deepest religious and moral convictions which we may hold absolutely are best expressed in language as encouragements to humility and further study and conversation about the deepest commitments of others.[19]

Notes

1. Madeleine Albright, Address to the American Academy of Religion (Washington, D.C., Nov.20, 2006).

2. Ronald Stone, "Ethics in Policy Making and the Implications for Theological Education," *The Christian Century* (April 23, 1969), 548–50.

3. Isaiah 2, Micah 4.

4. Edward L. Long, Jr., *Facing Terrorism*, 41–59.

5. Alan Geyer and Barbara Green, *Lines in the Sand* (Louisville; Westminster/John Knox Press, 1992).

6. Kenneth Vaux, *Ethics and the Gulf War* (Boulder: Westview Press, 1992).

7. Stone, *Prophetic Realism*, 162.

8. Vaux, 20.

9. Thomas L. Friedman, "The Case for Illegal Mingling: Islam Needs to find a way for its sects to get along," *Pittsburgh Post-Gazette* (Nov. 27, 2007) B9.

10. Thomas E. Ricks, *Fiasco: The American Military Adventure in Iraq* (New York: Penguin Books, 2007).179–82.

11. Richard Clarke, *Against All Enemies* (New York: Free Press, 2004).

12. See: Ricks, *Fiasco*.

13. See Alan Geyer and Barbara Green, *Line in the Sand* for a complete analysis of the first Iraq war in terms of just war concepts.

14. Stone, *Prophetic Realism*, 132–54.

15. See *Foreign Affairs* (July/August, 2007), 2–32.

16. She was quoted as saying: "We are going to support President Abbas and what he wants to do." *The New York Times* (June 19, 2007) 1.

17. See: Jim Holt, *The London Review of Books* (October 18, 2007).

18. Kenneth F. Sabine and Matthew J. Slaughter, "A New Deal for Globalization" in *Foreign Affairs* (July/August, 2007), 34–47, recognize the need for reforming globalization and adjusting American income if globalization is to continue.

19. A similar list of recommendations is found in Stanley Hoffmann, "The Foreign policy the United States Needs" in *The New York Review of Books* (April 10, 2006), 60–64. He puts a little more emphasis on international organizational reform and less on philosophy of morals, religion, and interreligious dialogue.

Index

~

About the Author

Ronald H. Stone retired from the John Witherspoon Chair of Ethics at Pittsburgh Theoilogical Seminary while continuing to serve as an adjunct professor of religion at the University of Pittsburgh. The thirty-four years of teaching social ethics in Pittsburgh were preceeded by short teaching terms at Vassar College, Union Theoligical Seminary, and an assistant professorship at Columbia University. He earned his Ph.D. at Columbia in ethics and international relations which included a year's study at Oxford University in moral philosophy.

He lectured and published internationally in Asia and Europe and traveled in Africa and Latin America while writing four previous books on ethics and international relations. The most recent is *Prophetic Realism: Beyond Militarism and Pacifism in an Age of Terror* (T&T Clark, 2005). His career produced some sixteen other academic books on peacemaking, politics, ethics, and intellectual biographies including several with the University Press of America and Rowman & Littlefield.

His experience as a scholar in world religions inspired him to engage in dialogue, lecturing, and preaching in countries behind the Iron Curtain in the Cold War from 1980–1989 and in the Middle East 1980–2006 meeting leaders in philosophy, religion, and government.

An activist in his early teaching years, he mellowed somewhat in retirement to participation in consulting with the Presbyterian Church's social, peacemaking work, occasional projects for the National Council of

Churches, World Council of Churches, and serving on Allegheny County's Accountability and Ethics Commission.

He continues to reside in Pittsburgh. His son, Randall, directs international relations studies at the University of Rochester, and his daughter, Patricia, an artist, coordinates the Media Center at the San Francisco College of Arts.